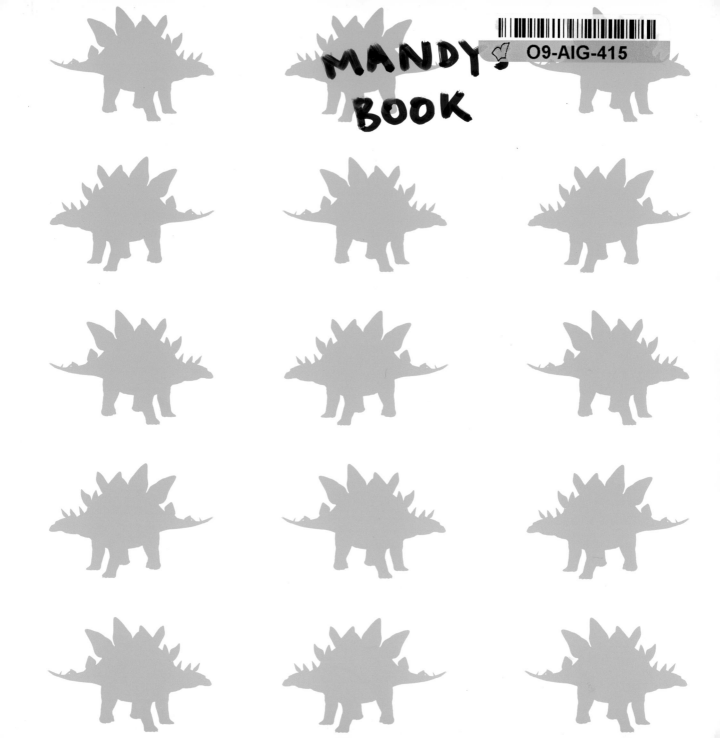

HOW TO KEEP
DINOSAURS

HOW TO KEEP
DINOSAURS

BY ROBERT MASH
FOREWORD BY RICHARD DAWKINS

WEIDENFELD & NICOLSON

Contents

*Page 2: There is an enormous
selection of small dinosaurs
suitable for today's pet-lover.
Left:* Coelophysis *(see p. 49)
enyoys a midnight snack, but
it cannot abide mushrooms.*

Foreword

Great humorists don't tell jokes. They plant new species of jokes and then help
them evolve, or just sit back and watch them self-propagate, grow and sprout again.

Stephen Potter's *Gamesmanship* is a single elaborated
joke, nurtured and sustained through *Lifemanship* and
One-Upmanship. The joke mutated and evolved with such
fertility that, far from fading with repetition, it grew and became
funnier. He helped it along by planting supporting memes:
'ploy' and 'gambit', the pseudo-academic footnotes, the fictitious
collaborators, Odoreida and Gattling-Fenn – who just might
not be fictitious. Now, thirty years after Potter's death, if I were
to coin, say, Postmodernship, or GM-manship, you would be
primed for the joke and ready to go one better. Most Jeeves
stories are mutants of one archetypal joke, and again it is a species
that evolves and matures to become more funny, not less, with
the retelling. The same could be said of *1066 and All That, The
Memoirs of an Irish RM*, and certainly *Lady Addle Remembers*.
How to Keep Dinosaurs belongs in that great tradition.

Ever since our student days together, Robert Mash has been
not just a humorist but a fecund propagator of new evolutionary
lineages of humour. If he had a predecessor, it was Psmith: 'That
low moaning sound you hear is the wolf bivouacked outside my
door' is what I would think of as a Mashian way of saying 'I'm
skint'. Psmithian, too, was Mash's grave response to a woman
who had just met him at a party. On learning that he was a
schoolmaster at a famous school, her innocent conversational
question was, 'And do you have girls?' His one word reply,
'Occasionally', was calculated to disconcert with exactly Psmith's
unblinking solemnity.

Mash's imaginative variants of 'Stap m'vitals' had his whole
circle of friends busy inventing new ones, which became ever
more bizarre as the species evolved through the memetic

microculture. The same for names of English pubs. The Rose
and Crown in Oxford was our local (where, indeed, much of
this early evolution took place) but it was seldom referred to so
straightforwardly. 'See you in The Cathedral and Gallbladder'
would have been heard somewhere along the evolutionary line.
Later specimens seem funny only within the context of their
evolutionary history. Another lineage that Mash planted was the
indefinitely evolving variant of the 'Our ... friend' convolution.
To begin with, 'Rose and Crown' might be 'Our floral regal
friend' but later descendants of the line evolved the baroque
crypticity of a crossword clue and needed a classical education
to decipher. The phylum to which all these Mashian species
of humour ultimately belonged could be called deadpan
circumlocution.

But the youthful Robert Mash as humorist belies the serious
scholar of his maturity. Nowhere is his serious side more evident
than in this book, where he brings together his lifelong expertise
on dinosaurs, their habits and maintenance, in sickness and in
health. His name has long been a byword in the dinosaur fancy.
From show-ring to auction-hall, from racecourse to pterosaur-
moor, no gathering of saurophiles is complete until the whisper
goes the rounds: 'Mash has arrived.' Even the carnosaurs seem
to sense the presence of the master and walk with an added
spring to their bipedal step, an added sneer to their bacteria-laced
jaws. He is ever ready with a reassuring pat to the diffident
hindquarters of a *Compsognathus* or timely advice to its owner.

Is your lap-dinosaur reaching that difficult (not to say
uncomfortable) age of needing a spur trim? Mash will advise you
on proper pruning before it all ends in tears and inadvertent (and

oh so well-meant) laparotomy. Is your gun-dinosaur becoming over-enthusiastic? Call Mash in before it 'retrieves' too many beaters (your retriever's mouth may be as soft as your ghillie's muffled cries for help, but there are limits to both). For those embarrassing moments, as when a *Microraptor* forgets it is in the drawing room, Mash's advice is as discreet as it is succinct. Or are you looking for a load of well-rotted *Iguanodon* manure for the smallholding? Mash is your man.

Though nowadays better known as sage elder statesman of the dinosaur fancy, Robert Mash has seen his share of action. Few who saw him 'up' will forget his insouciant seat on 'Killer', as he nursed that peerless hunter over the twenty-foot jumps to yet another clear round. As for dressage, under 'RM's' spirited martingale even a buck *Brachiosaurus* would prance like a thoroughbred *Ornithomimus*. His view halloo when whipping in that famous pack of twenty *Velociraptor* would quicken the pulse of any sportsman, and chill the already cold blood of the hapless *Bambiraptor* gone to ground. And when he donned his well-pounced leather, he was not to be snited at – indeed he was lucratively sought after as a consultant in Arabian royal houses. His freshly enseamed *Pterodactylus*, expertly cast off and with the wind in its sails, would ring up peerlessly before footing and trussing its *Archaeopteryx*, with a final, satisfying feake on the gauntlet.

For years, his many friends and admirers on the dinosaur circuit had urged Mash to set down his lifetime's experience in book form, as only he could. The first edition of *How to Keep Dinosaurs* was the result, and it predictably sold out quicker than the whipcrack of an *Apatosaurus* tail. Through the out-of-print wilderness years, well-thumbed bootleg copies became ever more prized possessions, jealously guarded in game bag or Range Rover glove pocket. The need for a second edition became pressing and I am delighted to have been instrumental, however indirectly, in helping to bring it about ('Whoso findeth a publisher findeth a good thing' – Proverbs 18:22). The second edition has, of course, benefited from Mash's tireless correspondence with dinosaur-owners the world over.

The book can be appreciated on many levels. It is by no means only an owner's manual, though it is indispensably that. For all its sound practical advice, it could only have been written by a professional zoologist, drawing deeply on theory and scholarship. Many of the facts herein are accurate. The world of dinosaurs has always been richly provided with wonder and amazement, and Mash's manual only adds to the mixture. As a theological aside, creationists (now excitingly rebranded as Intelligent Design Theorists) will find it an invaluable resource in their battle against the preposterous canard that humans and dinosaurs are separated by 65 million years of geological time.

As Robert Mash himself might warn, a dinosaur is for life (a very long life in the case of some sauropods) not just for Christmas. The same could be said of his book. Nevertheless, it will make a delightful present for anyone, of any age, and for many Christmases to come.

Richard Dawkins

Why Keep Dinosaurs?

Queen Victoria once said: 'When a man is tired of dinosaurs,
he is tired of life; for there is in a dinosaur all that life can afford'.

Enlightened and broad-minded as always, Victoria was trying to encourage the fashion for keeping dinosaurs which was just starting to spring up in her reign and had unfortunately produced some problems, including, in the Tay Bridge in Scotland, at least one disaster. Most of the difficulties were due to ignorance and self-confidence, both necessary in a successful imperial nation but often fatal in the more specialized field of dinosaur husbandry.

It all started in southern England: Mary Anning in Dorset and Thomas Hawkins in Somerset had been keeping marine reptiles such as *Icthyosaurus* and *Plesiosaurus* but Gideon Mantell and his wife Mary Ann in Sussex were the first to succeed with true dinosaurs. Although things went very well with ankylosaurs and *Iguanodon*, they failed spectacularly with *Megalosaurus* (Dr Mantell ended his life a cripple). In the capital Richard Owen was lending respectability to the hobby with his enormous collection in South Kensington. In the U.S.A., Timothy Matlack and Caspar Wistar were succeeding with hadrosaurs in New Jersey, while William Clark was having fun with dinosaurs in Montana. But it was not until the Frenchman Louis Dollo made his famous breakthrough by triumphantly keeping a herd of *Iguanodon* in a Belgian coal mine that dinosaur-keeping really became alive and took off.

With triumph came disaster. Ambitious entrepreneurs tried to do too much too quickly: what worked with *Iguanodon* didn't necessarily work with other dinosaurs, which often proved too big,

too fierce, too delicate or too possessive. The dinosaur bubble burst: animals were dumped from carts onto public highways or thrown into canals. The population was turning away from dinosaurs.

This was how things stood: before 1983 there was a small number of dedicated dinosaurophils, trying hard to keep dinosaurs but handicapped by ignorance, not only of the basics of dinosaur-keeping such as housing, feeding and breeding but also of how to obtain healthy specimens. In 1983 the first edition of this book was published and the rest is history. With the information, encouragement and advice contained herein, people of every nation have found the confidence to express themselves in the medium of mesozoic megapets: outlets have been established, clubs and societies have formed, information is being exchanged, misconceptions are being aborted and dinosaur-keeping is here to stay.

I intend this book mainly as a help to pet lovers who wish to keep a dinosaur or two in their house or garden, and are not quite sure how to go about it. I also talk about some species that are perhaps best left to large landowners or professionals who already have some experience of keeping animals that need lots of space. I hope to show you that, whereas most of the dinosaurs with which you may be already familiar are huge, there are many species that are small and manageable enough to be kept successfully, either as pets or for commercial purposes. This book deals with some of the

Dinosaur Icons *and what they mean*

Every entry in this book is accompanied by a set of icons that gives an at-a-glance description of each dinosaur.

Herbivore	*Insectivore*	*Omnivore*	*Fussy eater*	*Likes children*	*Likes children to eat*	*House trainable*	*Guard-dino*	*Worryingly stupid*

| *Carnivore* | *Pescivore* | *Easily fed* | *Will eat other pets* | *Iffy with babies* | *Suitable for domestic use* | *Trainable (does tricks)* | *Worryingly clever* | *Worryingly flatulent* |

better-known dinosaurs: although it is intended to encourage the beginner, I hope that some more experienced keepers will find something of value in it. In this second edition there are in most cases separate sections under each species where I have tried to suggest how to house and feed it and also, wherever this is feasible, how to breed it. Unfortunately, we do not yet know how to unlock the doors to the sex-life of some species, but dedicated fanciers are labouring night and day to find the key (or appropriate combination). A feature of this edition is the inclusion not only of photographs of all the featured species but also sensational scenes showing many of them together with their owners, at work and play, wonderful examples of how some of us are taking advantage of the opportunities afforded by these fascinating pets and work-place colleagues.

I have included some animals (thecodonts, weigeltisaurs and pterosaurs) that are not, strictly speaking, dinosaurs at all; this is, after all, a practical manual rather than a taxonomic treatise. A simple classification of the dinosaurs may be found on page 94. The dinosaurs proper, including both the Orders Saurischia and Ornithischia contain as varied a group of animals as can be imagined. They range in size from the rabbit-sized *Compsognathus* to *Brachiosaurus* (50 tons) and *Diplodocus* (27 metres/89 feet). There are stupid ones like *Stegosaurus* and intelligent ones like *Troodon*. Some, like *Iguanodon*, are vegetarian; others, such as *Ceratosaurus*, will only eat meat. The brontosaurs are ponderous

and slow, but *Struthiomimus* can race along at 80 kilometres (50 miles) per hour. *Sordes* (a pterosaur) is covered in fur, *Archaeopteryx* in feathers, *Polacanthus* in spines and *Nodosaurus* in warts. *Anatosaurus* is mild and gentle; *Tyrannosaurus* is lethal.

If you have never kept dinosaurs you may well ask: 'Why bother?' Well, as you can see, dinosaurs are a fascinatingly varied group of animals. I cannot recommend the biggest as domestic pets, but the small ones, and some of the thecodonts, will fit perfectly into any home as long as the owner takes a few elementary precautions. Some of them need no special housing and can live on household scraps; others can be trained as guard 'dogs' and used by police and other security organizations. Indeed, the most imaginative among military experts can see their deployment as tactical weapons, particularly in warm climates. Some are ideal for recreation, with riding and hunting obvious examples; dinosaurs may be farmed for their eggs, their feathers, their hides and their meat; they may be used on farms as tractors, sheep-dinos or JCBs. The wealthy and status-conscious may keep them in their extensive parks; the less wealthy will charge you to walk with them or ride on them; zoos and safari parks will display them in their glory for your pleasure. A further attraction of the dinosaurs is that, in these conservation-conscious days, the keeping of rare or threatened species is rightly frowned upon: no such qualms can hinder the dinosaur-keeper, who deals only with animals that are already extinct.

Extra
security

Government
license necessary

Noisy

Kleptomaniac

Indiscriminate
courtship

Vitamin supplement
neccesary in winter.

Messy
moulter

scale

weight

Extreme
security

Nocturnal

Bites!

Burrower/
digger

Climate
sensitive

Regular
grooming

Suffers travel
sickness

location

A Dinosaur-Keeper's Basic Toolkit...

Before you get your first dinosaur, there are a few basic tools that you will need to make sure that your pet feels comfortable in his new home.

City-bound dinosaurs are particularly prone to skin complaints, which may require chemical treatment.

A stout shovel is a useful ally for the owner of the larger dinosaur.

Make sure you have adequate equipment for the restraint of your beast. If all else fails, it often pays to have a tranquilizer rifle at the ready.

Reinforced gauntlets are crucial when attempting to feed a sick dinosaur its antibiotic pills, or when taking its temperature.

Private owners of Velociraptor and Deinonychus are legally required to trim their pets' disembowelling claws.

Larger species will need vast quantities of food. Make sure this won't be a problem!

Unfortunately, it is often necessary to take the temperature of sickening or broody dinosaurs.

Sensible, protective head gear is a must for dealing with all species of ankylosaur.

Good, stiff brushes will keep your dinosaur's scales in tip-top condition. You may also choose to apply one of the many brands of dinosaur wax available.

Remember that some carnivores will only eat fresh meat. Particularly fussy dinosaurs will insist on it being served alive...

1 | DINOSAURS FOR BEGINNERS

Given the range of dinosaurs now available, the first time owner can be tempted to bite off more than they can chew (a problem, alas, not always faced by their pet of misguided choice). With this in mind, here are three dinosaurs you just can't go wrong with.

An English proverb from the fourteenth century tells us: 'Everything must have a beginning'. Those of us who are not quantum physicists would probably agree. Euripides, seventeen centuries earlier, went further when he said: 'A bad beginning makes a bad ending'. Another more positive fourteenth-century English proverb put it: 'A good beginning makes a good ending'. What dinosaur, then, should the beginner start with?

What should you avoid? The icons by each dinosaur entry will be useful here: if you are new to dinosaur-keeping these will help you to avoid some of the more obvious problems. For instance, don't even think of a pet that needs 'security measures', whether 'special' or 'extreme'; if you live in a small apartment or bungalow, keep away from the 'worryingly flatulent' animal; if you live outside the tropics, have nothing to do with 'climate sensitive' creatures; if you sleep at night, avoid the 'nocturnal' ones. In other words, use your common sense. What sort of housing is needed? A suburban back garden is no place for a herd of *Triceratops.*

What should you choose? Go for the icons that tell you that your pet will be 'suitable for domestic use', 'house-trainable' (if you're fussy) and 'trainable (will do tricks)'. If you have special needs, perhaps your new pet will come in handy: for example the lonely (for whatever reason) might be attracted to *Stegoceras* (for whatever reason), or the malevolent to one of the smaller raptors. Do you wish to impress the neighbours, or would you prefer new ones? You will need to consider all these questions, and many others, before you make your final decision.

History is littered with cases where otherwise sensible people have bitten off more than they can chew and come off the rails, usually in that order. Nowhere is this more true than on the long and hard track that is dinosaur-keeping. We remember with pity the disillusioned dairy farmer looking for diversification who didn't think before acquiring a herd of *Iguanodon*; we recall the penniless earl who, relying on a thousand years of history, failed to think before acting on the impulse to stock his stately acres with brachiosaurs. We must always remember that nobody ever got anywhere by inviting *Tyrannosaurus rex* into his town house. The prospective dinosaurist must ignore what attracted him to dinosaurs in the first place, and think small. He should recall the wise words of Matthew Henry in his commentaries on the Book of Genesis: 'Many a dangerous temptation comes to us in gay, fine colours, that are but skin deep'.

For those who still cannot make up their minds I have chosen three starters: *Euparkeria*, *Coelurosauravus* and *Compsognathus*. Although challenging, they are all within anyone's capacity to manage and cherish and, while they may have some surprising quirks, they will prepare you for later, greater things should you decide that size matters.

For practical reasons there is nothing better for beginners to cut their teeth on than a thecodont such as *Euparkeria*. Not a true dinosaur, I admit, but a step up from the reptiles you might normally keep. There are many technical definitions of dinosaurs, usually involving bones of the skull or hips, but the best working definition involves the legs: does the object of your admiration and affection have 'improved legs'? By this I mean the fundamental evolutionary step of having the legs below the body, as in mammals, rather than sticking out sideways, as in reptiles. This single design enhancement, by improving the efficiency of their posture and locomotion, was responsible for the success of the dinosaurs. *Euparkeria* is halfway there, resting sprawled out like a reptile, but running with legs tucked under, like a real dinosaur. If you are already happy in the company of reptiles, *Euparkeria* is only a little different, but after only a few days in your care you will already begin to notice the difference: *Euparkeria* is already showing, in embryonic form, those rudiments of the polish, intellect, individuality and sheer endosauropsidity of the world of the dinosaur.

For those whose bent is more aerial I have chosen *Coelurosauravus*. Like *Euparkeria*, it is a reptile with aspirations to greater things. If you intend to specialize in pterosaurs, then it is probably a good idea to start with this little creature, rather than go down the road of flying foxes and vampires. To begin with, it is smaller than most pterosaurs and therefore more manageable, and its housing requirements are simpler. It is happy indoors and will furnish the whole family with endless hours of fun. Furthermore, there are none of the tedious problems connected with keeping the food warm and uncoagulated, as there are with vampire culture.

Finally, we arrive at *Compsognathus*. Everyone wants a compy, but supplies are limited: Germany is the place to go for the best specimens and real bargains can be obtained in the relaxed commercial intercourse characteristic of the later stages of the various beer festivals in Bavaria. The thing about compies is that they are real dinosaurs, showing all the fascination, wit and invention that we have come to expect from these prehistoric peaches. Keep one in your apartment, keep a dozen in your mansion; feed them on mice, let them eat cats; give them to your granny for fun, lend them to your neighbours for games: *Compsognathus* is the ideal first dinosaur for everyone.

What, then, is the snag? Why don't all dinosaur lovers keep compies? Agile, lively, beautiful, it would seem an ideal animal for the collection. It fails, alas, the test that so many people set for their dinosaur: it doesn't get big. If you want your brute big, a compy doesn't quite measure up to the task. If we are to be frank, we must admit that *Compsognathus* is but a step on the way to the real thing. Before we can carry our brontosaur bride over the threshold of dinosaur husbandry we must plod steadfastly along the prosaic path of euparkerian pleasure, swim in the shallow sea of coelurosauravian self-indulgence or lie on the couch of compy contentment.

Compsognathus

'WELL-DRESSED JAW', from Greek κομΨος *(well-dressed)* + γναθος *(jaw), from a Chinese recipe.*

Perfect for city dwellers, chicken-sized, gentle, loving and easily house-trained, and fine with children. Should suit small family in a centrally-heated apartment.

The compy is about 70 centimetres (28 inches) long, with grasping fingers. Like so many coelurosaurs, it has hollow bones filled with air, so that it is very light and extremely agile. There are several species, and colours vary from one to another, tending towards the gaudy, with oranges and greens predominating.

A compy is the ideal dinosaur for city dwellers. It is hardy and adaptable. Once it learns to recognize its owner it is mild-mannered and affectionate.

A form with malformed hands is sometimes marketed as *Compsognathus corallestris*: it is said to swim and dive, but I have yet to see one that flourished on the seafood diet that is recommended for it.

Feeding: *Compsognathus* is carnivorous, feeding on mammals, lizards, insects, small pterosaurs – anything it can get its hands on. It prefers its food alive, and if you give your compies an animate diet, they prosper more and are more likely to breed than those brought up on scraps and corpses.

Housing: It is small enough to share an apartment or a small house, and, if encouraged from the outset, can often be house-trained, especially if you can induce it to use its own lavatory area. It is perfectly safe with children (though perhaps a bit iffy with babies), but its grasping fingers are often a nuisance in well-furnished houses, so that a degree of confinement may be needed.

Breeding: Breeding is no problem so long as the couple are given some privacy.

Temperature is a releaser of breeding behaviour in your compies. If they steadfastly refuse to copulate (in extreme cases, even to court), raising the temperature by a couple of degrees will usually work; if not, spraying the animals with warm water may do the trick. Try them both (raised temperature and spray) together.

Space is needed by dinosaurs just as much as time is needed by Englishmen: infertile females become fecund and moping males make more effort when extra acres are added to their playgrounds. Feeding may be crucial. A high-protein diet is often advised before breeding and this applies just as much to dinosaurs. Do not let males eat too much food: too much starch and not enough exercise fattens them, so that copulation, always a hit or miss affair, becomes impossible.

The period of laying and incubation is always difficult. Give the hens as much isolation and quiet as possible and keep the cocks away. Disturb the sitting dinosaur as little as you can: the more disturbance, the greater the likelihood of eggs being trodden on.

Availability: Generally available from the usual Dinomarts; bargains can be had from booths in the Bavarian Beer Festivals and also from travelling salesmen in parts of southeast France.

2.5kg
5.5lb

Left: Your compies can, with perseverance, be trained to use a litter tray.

Euparkeria

'GOOD PARKER', from Greek εύ (good) + Latin parkeria (parker), because it is so easy to find room for.

For the beginner or experienced reptile-keeper, the classical first step on the romantic road of dinosaur-keeping. Active, small, manageable and easily fed on scraps.

If you are used to keeping reptiles such as iguanas, you should definitely start your dinosaur collection with a thecodont: I warmly recommend *Euparkeria* as an alternative to *Compsognathus*. *Euparkeria* is an ornithosuchian, and as such marks a border line between reptiles and dinosaurs proper. The ornithosuchians' principle virtue is their relatively small size (not necessarily a virtue to the dedicated dinosaurophil!) and consequent manageability.

Euparkeria is about 60 centimetres (24 inches) long and to most tastes an attractive animal, although, like many objects of enduring appeal, it may take some getting used to. Your first sight of a *Euparkeria* will almost certainly be when it is resting or walking on all fours, when its legs are spread out sideways like a lizard's; however, once the creature is running, its hind legs move under the body to give it that speed and support that is so much a part of their function. In other respects *Euparkeria* looks a bit like an iguana.

There is a curious lump between the front of the head and the eyes, which contains what seems to be some sort of gland: it is not yet known what this is for, so there is an opportunity here for amateur natural historians to undertake some research. Indeed, ambitious parents will appreciate that in an age when opportunities for this type of really useful research are increasingly hard to find a child who grows up with *Euparkeria* in the house may well be on a winner when the time for doctoral theses comes around.

Like *Coelurosauravus* (p. 17), *Euparkeria* grows to be affectionate and keen on company. My own pet, Dorothy, long dead, loved to be patted and stroked, especially with a fingernail drawn sensuously back from the tip of the nose, across the forehead and skull, and on down to the nape of the neck. For most specimens, two minutes of this makes them positively glow with satisfaction

and take on a facial expression that some fanatics describe as 'smiling'. Sadly, this is a euphemism. The 'smile' of the hypercontented *Euparkeria* closely resembles the anticipatory leer of the human psychopath: the hooded eyelids droop, rendering the eyes barely visible, the upper lips retract, revealing the pointed teeth, the jaw drops open and the tongue lolls from side to side.

The uninitiated should not be introduced to a *Euparkeria* in this state. However, the smiles of this lovable ornithosuchian, like those of presidents and prime ministers the world over, are another aspect of the animal that its supporters quickly get used to and ignore.

Feeding: *Euparkeria* is a true carnivore and most individuals must have a diet consisting largely of cold meat. Feed it on cat-food, meat (cold) and scraps.

Housing: They are mostly naked, without fur or feathers, and therefore need fairly warm quarters.

Breeding: As iguanas.

Availability: As *Compsognathus* (see p. 15).

Coelurosauravus

'LONELY WOMB-TAIL LIZARD-BIRD', from Greek κοιλια *(womb)* + ούρα *(tail)* + σαυρος *(lizard) + Latin* avius *(lonely), from a mistaken belief that it reproduced in an unusual and unpopular way.*

A gliding conversation piece and a perfect first dinosaur. A cage in a warm room and the usual cat-foods are all that *Coelurosauravus* needs; in summer it can go outdoors.

Coelurosauravus is, of course, a reptile, not a dinosaur. It is, in fact, a small gliding weigeltisaurid with a thin membrane of skin stretched over long rods that grow from the side of the body. It maintains stability by means of the long tail stretching out behind. The hind legs control gliding and, because the membrane is elastic, *Coelurosauravus* has a fairly controlled 'flight', rather like that of Leadbeater's Possum (*Gymnobelidius*). Also like that marsupial, it cannot 'flap' its 'wings' and 'fly' properly: it must glide down from a higher point to a lower one.

Although shy by nature, *Coelurosauravus* – particularly those kept singly – grow to adore human company and can become extremely affectionate. They enjoy being stroked and will sit on your shoulders for hours if you let them. In fact, it can sometimes be quite difficult to get them off; if you cannot tempt them away by food, there are two other ruses that generally work. One is to climb to the top of a very tall tree and then begin to climb down again; at this point *Coelurosauravus* will realize that he is in danger of missing the opportunity for an especially long and satisfying glide and will gently disengage and float away. You must then stay in the tree until your pet has landed, either on the ground or on someone else, for if you come down too quickly, *Coelurosauravus* may make a slow circular descent, carefully timed to coincide with your own return to ground level. Athletic owners may at first find this an amusing game and source of exercise, but it is definitely not to be encouraged.

The less dangerous alternative is to invest in a dressmaker's dummy or a shop-window-type mannequin and always to wear a jacket that you don't mind taking off and leaving.

Feeding: *Coelurosauravus* is omnivorous, with a preference for animal matter; it will usually take cat-foods but often rejects dog-foods.

Housing: Give it an enclosure wired in on all sides and on top; remember it is a climber and can easily glide out if you have no roof. Give it shrubs or, better still, a tree or two to climb about in, though if you provide too many tall trees you may never see this charming but shy creature, as it hides in the foliage. You can allow your *Coelurosauravus* the freedom of most rooms in the house. It will have a natural inclination to climb any convenient drapes or curtains and to float spectacularly down at its leisure. Since it does not flap its 'wings', the gliding process is completely silent. It is, therefore, a good idea to warn visitors – especially elderly relatives and nervous individuals – of its presence, as tame specimens love to alight on the shoulders, or sometimes the heads, of anyone passing by.

Breeding: No information currently available. In spite of its name, it is believed to lay eggs in the traditional way.

Availability: Can be obtained, at exorbitant cost, from the usual retail outlets in Madagascar; you can also get them, relatively cheaply, from various European Internet sites.

2 | DINOSAURS AS HOUSE PETS

When you've cut your teeth on little gems like *Compsognathus* you will be, not ready – nobody's ever really ready for dinosaurs – but better prepared to take on some proper beauties.

After visiting relatives who keep real dinosaurs (something a bit more challenging than compies) you may well contemplate acquiring some of your own. If you seek inspiration from the prophets of the Old Testament, ignore the words of the austere Zechariah: 'What are these wounds in thine hands? Then he shall answer, Those with which I was wounded in the house of my friends'; instead, think positive like Haggai: 'The glory of this house shall be greater than of the former'. There are risks, of course, but there are also rewards. A man without a dinosaur is like a snail without a love-dart.

The following section suggests half a dozen dinosaurs that can, with only a few adjustments to your normal patterns of living, become welcome parts of your household; there is also one to be wary of.

Podokesaurus: a warning

In the first edition of this book I suggested that *Podokesaurus* was 'a pretty little theropod, easily fed and good with children'. In a sense this was true: the animal that was all too often described as *Podokesaurus* was pretty and little, and easily fed, but it was a mistake to suggest that it was good with children: the phrase should have read '...easily fed and likes children': unfortunately, too many, perhaps all, of the *Podokesaurus* that were kept turned out to be juvenile forms of *Coelophysis* (p. 48), and although they flourished in the company of children, the reverse could not be said to be the case. Although there were some unfortunate accidents involving total or partial consumption of juvenile owners, in most cases there was no more than loss of fingers and parts of arms (and, in a few probably rather exaggerated cases, whole limbs). Nonetheless, in spite of the continuing huge discounts ('two for the price of one' and so on), this is a dinosaur that is, like *Coelophysis*, more suited to police work than the nursery.

So what dinosaurs are suited to the nursery? There are many, many dinosaurs that are suitable for the home and family, but you have to be very careful where babies are concerned: the more intelligent dinosaurs tend to be carnivores and the more gentle dinosaurs tend to be clumsy. Many parents are understandably upset when their babies are eaten or crushed, so you must be prudent in your choice. My own recommendation is to keep the nursery a dinosaur-free zone or, better still, keep dinosaurs out of the home until the children are big enough to look after themselves in what may well be a vigorous and uncompromising environment. That said, there are many dinosaurs that may well fit in the family environment, after suitable training. *Thecodonto-saurus*, for example, although rather slow-witted, is very good with children; so are *Incisivosaurus* and *Microraptor* and, when it can be torn away from the television, *Heterodontosaurus*.

What about the adults in the family? In this age of carbohydrates, television and obesity I have good news for fatties. One of the reasons people don't take as much exercise as they should is because it is so boring. But with a dinosaur to accompany you you can say goodbye to the joylessness of jogging and the weariness of working out: *Thecodontosaurus* will happily join you in your run, matching you stride for stride and turning your previous dreary duty into fun, fun, fun. Fun for you, fun for your dinosaur and fun for the other joggers. If you are committed to the life out of doors, whether as a cross-country runner or a less lively hiker, there is a dinosaur for you: *Fabrosaurus*. Like *Thecodonto-saurus*, it is by no means the sharpest pin in the cushion but will match whatever pace you choose and has the stamina to keep right on to the end of the road.

Many people keep dogs or cats for company. Dinosaurs, too, can be a consolation for the lonely. If you are not yet ready to commit yourself to an exclusive relationship, then *Leptoceratops* is certainly worth a try. There are snags, of course; nobody has yet managed to house-train *Leptoceratops*, and a great deal of room is needed if the dinosaur is to be really happy in the relationship. But with give and take on both sides, together with plenty of tissues or, better still, bales of straw, a fulfilling temporary relationship can usually be built up between the two of you. For the more serious fancier there can be no better partner than *Stegoceras*: here, in spite of inevitable mutual nervousness at first, there is every possibility of an ongoing and meaningful lifelong relationship, as long as you keep the dinosaur's feet warm and dry.

In most homes the relationship with the resident dinosaur is likely to prove much more easy-going and, if not exactly impersonal, at least semi-detached. All the dinosaurs in the section that follows are capable of forming decorous attachments, although *Stegoceras* will sometimes have to be handled sensitively. The problems that you will encounter are usually easy enough to solve: *Incisivosaurus*'s tendency to chew things; *Microraptor*'s love of climbing; the problems encountered when *Heterodontosaurus* is courting.

In the end, it all comes down to common sense, yet again. Do you have the space to accommodate your pet? Are you able to feed it properly? Can you keep it warm and happy? Can you cope with its personality? Will it get on with the children, and they with it? If the answers to these questions are yes, yes, yes, yes and probably, then you are, as they say, ready to roll.

Remember to scan the icons with care and choose accordingly. If you get this decision right, then you are well on the way to playing with the big boys. And girls.

Left: Podokesaurus,
aka Coelophysis.

Microraptor

'SMALL THIEF', from Greek μικρος *(small) + Latin* raptor *(thief).*

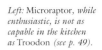

Left: Microraptor, *while enthusiastic, is not as capable in the kitchen as* Troodon *(see p. 49).*

Our smallest dinosaur, a tiny version of *Velociraptor*, tameable, trainable, loveable and easy-to-feed; easily kept in a small house or medium-sized conservatory, where its ready intelligence makes it a fairly safe pet for adventurous and modern children.

With a body no longer than 20 centimetres (8 inches) and the rest tail, *Microraptor* is covered all over with dinofuzz – long, thin, feathery filaments. Despite its cuddly looks, it is basically ferocious but can easily be tamed and trained. Children adore *Microraptor* and it adores them, liking nothing better than to be hugged, squeezed, carried, put to bed, pushed around on tricycles and to join in on any fun that's going. It also makes a very suitable lap pet for the increasing number of adults who have nothing better to do than sit around with dinosaurs in their laps. Be warned: its name means small thief – lock up your valuables!

Feeding: It is easily fed: like cats, *Microraptor* likes mice, but it will also eat most cat- and dog-foods.

Housing: *Microraptor* is a climbing dinosaur and needs perches or branches to clamber about on. You can give it the run of your house, but it will climb the curtains and swing from the light-fixtures. A centrally-heated conservatory containing a few medium-sized trees makes an ideal home for your mini-dino.

Breeding: Not yet bred. Attempts in China to cross it with a bird seem to have failed.

Availability: You can now obtain them from the Yixian Formation Trading House, Liaoning, China.

Thecodontosaurus

'COFFIN-TUSK LIZARD', from Greek θηκη *(coffin) +* όδους, *(tooth) +* σαυρος *(lizard), from its habit of losing its teeth after colliding with upright objects such as gravestones.*

All the desirable dinosaurian qualities and none of the inconveniences. Large enough to impress your neighbours but small enough to be manageable.

Most of this animal's length is tail and much of the rest is neck. Its shape is almost classically brontosaurian but it is free of the random exuberance that spoils so many of those large vegetarians. It enjoys walking and runs in an unusual, very flat-footed manner, faintly reminiscent of Charlie Chaplin hurrying on all fours. You would be advised to keep it on a leash in towns and probably at all times, because it is likely to get lost and, indeed, due to its extremely short memory, to forget who its owner is. It is frankly rather a stupid animal, and you will not be able to train it to do anything useful. Concentrate on getting it to remember its own name, which should be as

short as possible, such as 'Hey', 'You' or 'Liz'. It is affectionate, good with children and, for a dinosaur, easy to manage.

Feeding: Give it plenty of green and root vegetables.

Housing: In summer it can stay outside in a large garden or paddock; in winter give it a spare room or a heated outhouse and exercise it every day.

Breeding: No information available.

Availability: In Britain, most easily obtained from the Thecodontostore in Bristol. Foreign buyers will probably need to get their specimens from Northeast Australia, as South African specimens usually turn out to be *Anchisaurus*.

Stegoceras

'Horny roof', from Greek στεγος (roof) + κερας (horn), from its habit of butting its sexual partner.

For the person who would like a friendly and inoffensive pet, pretty and easily fed, *Stegoceras* is ideal, as long as its feet are not allowed to stay wet.

When fully grown, these pretty little creatures are generally about the height of a woman. They are also bipedal and pleasingly sociable. They therefore make most interesting pets because they can walk beside you on approximately equal terms. Moreover, they will happily hold hands. They are particularly recommended for lonely people, and there is an opportunity here for the imaginative entrepreneur: breed yourself a herd, take the prettiest one with you and collect orders from the unfortunates who come out of singles bars on their own.

Of all the dinosaurs *Stegoceras* is perhaps most likely to become in time the smart pet. It is, after all, much more interesting than either an alligator or a rottweiler, and even tarantulas will be old hat. Of course, when this happens there is a danger that celebrities will want to put clothes on them and take them around in private jets. I have no evidence, but I have a feeling this might be a little too much for *Stegoceras* and could lead to neurosis and the whole gamut of anxiety-induced illnesses. It could provoke a regression to the wild state, even in those bred in domesticity. A non-house-trained *Stegoceras* would retain very little chic.

We must remember that, despite its humanoid stance, *Stegoceras* is a bone-headed dinosaur in every respect. The 12-centimetre- (5-inch-) thick dome of solid bone at the top of the head protects a brain not much more than 5 centimetres (2 inches) long. However, there is an attractive bony frill at the back of the head.

Keep its feet warm, or it is very likely to catch cold. Look carefully for any slightly unusual behaviour patterns such as shivering or unexpected vertical jumps. The most immediate cure is to swab the throat with eucalyptus. You may notice that one day your otherwise not unduly lascivious *Stegoceras* is giving you saucy winks. Fortunately, this is not what it seems: it is only the onset of a disease, peculiar to *Stegoceras* and a few other dinosaurs, known as 'One-eyed Cold' (see p. 93), whose main symptom is the frequent closing of one eye. Isolate the dinosaur immediately and cure with heat treatment. This is also good for dinosaur asthma (see p. 92), which occasionally attacks the more sensitive and less intelligent herbivores such as *Stegoceras*, particularly when they have experienced difficulty in making a decision. Never give them a choice of foods.

Feeding: As far as feeding is concerned, think of *Stegoceras* as a sheep that eats everything that a sheep eats except grass.

Housing: Think of *Stegoceras* as a sheep without wool: be sure to keep it warm.

Breeding: The exact mechanism remains uncertain, but eggs are laid in spring.

Availability: The Belly River Formation Dancing School, Alberta is the best source of this popular pachycephalosaurid.

Right: Stegoceras *makes a useful caddy as long you can accept the occasional tussle in the rough as par for the course.*

Heterodontosaurus

*'HETERO TOOTH-LIZARD', from Greek ετερος + όδους (tooth) + σαυρος (lizard),
after the male's tendency to bite other males.*

A very interesting, lively and
easily satisfied dinosaur,
Heterodontosaurus is
affectionate and well-disposed.
It is often called the rich man's
Fabrosaurus. It can easily
become part of the family.

Heterodontosaurus is about a metre (3 ¼
feet) long and, unless it's in a hurry, it goes
around on all fours. It is like *Fabrosaurus* in many
other ways, although it is more delicate and, it must
be said, more of a nuisance. Its grasping hands and
grasping feet tend to clutch anything within reach in
the home: this makes it more interesting to visitors
than to owners.

It is, however, affectionate as well as lively.
Children love to cuddle it and there is no reason
why they shouldn't, as long as they don't mind being
licked in return. The end of a child's bed is as good
a place for the creature to sleep as any.

Heterodontosaurus is fascinated by television and
this is a sure way to create a hiatus in its incessant
picking up and dropping of valuable objects. It is
totally transfixed by all sport and much comedy
(try it on *Buffy the Vampire Slayer*), and will
snuggle down goggle-eyed with child or adult.
Some specimens, the Albert Einsteins of their species,
can use a joystick well enough to play the simpler
computer games. The downside of this skill is that
many of them become addicted to the game and
refuse to give up the controls when it's someone
else's turn, or when it's time to go to bed. The
males are much more of a problem than the females
and it may be necessary to put on your protective
gear (see under 'Breeding', below) in order to wrest
the joystick from their uncompliant hands.
Feeding: It is herbivorous and easily satisfied. As
far as food goes, it is like *Fabrosaurus*: if a goat
will eat it, so will *Heterodontosaurus*. In addition,
Heterodontosaurus has no problems with
honeysuckle.

Housing: In the home, like a dog.
Breeding: The cock is a bit of a handful at mating
time and may need to be kept under firm control.
Although he is usually mild, he will unhesitatingly
use his 'canines' to attack rivals; as he is not good
at telling the difference between rivals and other
moving objects, he may well wound female and
owner alike in his vague but intense aggressive sexual
frenzy. If you are a serious breeder, you will find that
some form of leg protection is useful: spats, gaiters,
baseball or cricket pads – assemble whatever you
can. Equipment for dinosaur enthusiasts may soon
become big business: one of the first items on sale
will be protective leggings for *Heterodontosaurus*
breeders.
Availability: There are no problems in getting hold
of specimens but they have to be imported from
Cape Province in South Africa; you may be able to
pick up specimens from market stalls in Lesotho.

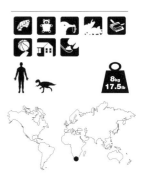

Fabrosaurus

'FABRE'S LIZARD', Fabre + Greek σαυρος (lizard), after Jean-Henri Fabre, who used his familiarity with their habits to oppose the theory of evolution.

Undemanding and amiable, *Fabrosaurus* is easily fed and will live happily in the house during the winter and with your goats in the garden during the summer.

Fabrosaurus is about a metre (3 ¼ feet) long and has long, slender back legs: it is, in fact, mainly bipedal and a good runner. It is sure-footed and has stamina, and is therefore especially recommended for hikers and cross-country walkers. In all, it is a fairly amiable little animal, but not very bright: in fact, it is pretty dim, but room may be found in most households for fancied individuals. If your *Fabrosaurus* is very intellectually challenged, it makes sense for both of you to wear brightly coloured and distinctive waistcoats when you run together, in case either of you gets lost.

Feeding: It has a horny beak, which it uses for cropping tough plants. It is very undemanding and loves to chew anything.

Housing: Think of it as a little goat, although, unlike a goat, *Fabrosaurus* has no hair and so needs heated quarters in winter. It will live contentedly enough in the house, although no one has managed yet to house-train it. Try wiring off a corner of the kitchen right up to the ceiling, because *Fabrosaurus* can climb!

Breeding: Reports of some success in South Africa.

Availability: The Red Beds Fabrostore in Lesotho is still the only means of getting specimens.

Leptoceratops

'SUBTLE HORNY EYE', from Greek λεπτος (subtle) + κερας (horn) + ωψ (eye), from its flirtatious nature.

If you have a small paddock, *Leptoceratops* is a very feasible ceratopian for you. It is easily fed and housed – and suited to captivity.

Leptoceratops is about 2 metres (6 ½ feet) long; it is bipedal, an agile runner and, although a Horned Dinosaur, unhorned. It is tricky to tame and, so far, impossible to house-train. A muzzle is recommended when you bring *Leptoceratops* into the house, not in itself recommended unless the furniture is screwed to the floor. *Leptoceratops* has longer arms than you would expect to find on a dinosaur that runs on its hind legs, and is very good at grabbing anything it fancies. Mature females are very flirtatious and can become so fond of their owners that you may need to think seriously about how far you want the relationship to go. A muzzle is essential and you may need to take other precautions.

Feeding: It will accept much the same diet as recommended for its larger relatives (see *Triceratops*, p. 80) but prefers softer food than they do.

Housing: Provide at least ¼ hectare (½ acre) of land for this dinosaur, because it needs fresh vegetation and, like penurious literati, is happiest when browsing.

Breeding: No one, as far as I have been able to discover, has bred these creatures, in spite of their pert natures: they are consequently in fairly short supply. This is a pity, as it means that many prospective owners turn to the easier, but less interesting, *Protoceratops* (p. 57).

Availability: The usual Dinomarts of Alberta in Canada and Wyoming in the U.S.A. are now being undercut in price by traders in the Mongolian markets.

Incisivosaurus

'CUTTING LIZARD', Mediaeval Latin incisivus *(cutting, penetrating with a sharp edge) + Greek* σαυρος *(lizard), for obvious reasons.*

An advanced dinosaur that is suitable for a child, in spite of its cousins. What a little gem!

Incisivosaurus, or bunnysaurus, as it is almost universally known, is relatively new on the dinosaur scene, specimens only recently becoming available on the Chinese market or, to be more accurate, in the Chinese market, as these little beauties are being smuggled in illegally and sold for the pot on the streets. Delicious they may be on the palate, but they are even more so in the home as pets and companions.

The official name *Incisivosaurus* refers to the two big, flat teeth in the front of the jaw: these look just like a rabbit's 'buck teeth' or incisors, and are used for cutting. Like the more familiar furry bunny rabbit, it is a gnawer, as owners of furniture and carpets have all too often found out, all too often too late! It is for this reason that bunnysaurus is not in the 'Dinosaurs for Beginners' section: in all other respects, it is a perfect beginner's dinosaur: easily fed, cuddly, loving and tolerant of abuse by children.

Is it safe with babies? The answer is a resounding yes! It is perhaps the only dinosaur that can be left alone with an infant in complete safety. It will always run to find the parents when it detects that a nappy needs changing: because bunnysaurus is too small to reach the doorhandle, you must always leave the doors to the baby's room open, as the conscientious dinosaur will gnaw its way from there to where the parents are. If you are lucky, it will make its route through the doors; but if it is in a hurry, it may gnaw directly through the walls. The wise parent will provide 'cat' flaps into every room in the house.
Feeding: Although your supplier will insist that you can make bunnysaurus happy with a vegetable diet, you will probably find that it has its own diet agenda.
Housing: In one sense it is easily housed: any cage, such as that used by your wombat, will be comfortable and even luxurious, but not, unfortunately, secure. Its buck teeth are not there just to improve its looks: they are there to gnaw. *Rodo ergo sum*, it seems to say (though probably in Mandarin). In practical terms, this means that it will gnaw its way out of almost any normal cage or container, however sturdy. Once out, it will gnaw its way into the home; once in, it will content itself with the destruction of only one or two items of furniture (keep a stock of unwanted chairs and tables that can be 'sacrificed' each time it enters) and then it will settle down with a nice bone, if you can find one for it. Cuttle bones are too flimsy. Give it something really substantial to gnaw: a cow's pelvis will keep it happy for hours.

The problem is supermarkets: they are not bunnysaurus-secure, and if there is one nearby your pet will gnaw its way into it, choose an item, usually hard and chewy, and bring it to be gnawed in the comfort and security of your own home.

What is the answer? Your problem can often be sorted out with glass: bunnysaurus finds supercooled liquids a problem and will usually concede defeat if your container is wholly glass (don't use angle-iron).
Breeding: Has only been achieved with escaped specimens, but extremely successful.
Availability: Chinese markets, especially rural.

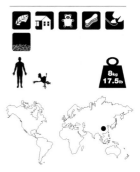

Left: Incisivosaurus *cannot resist a tug-of-war.*

3 | DINOSAURS AS FLYING PETS

Although most dinosaur-keepers are recruited from the ranks of herpetologists, a significant number are fond of birds, and want their hobby to reflect this leaning. If you want your dinosaurs to dive and soar, you need look no further than the pterosaurs and *Archaeopteryx*: these may not be dinosurs in the strictest sense, but life is too short for taxonomic pedants.

Pterosaurs are warm-blooded and most of them are furry. Many have teeth but some have lost them. Their most obvious feature is the membrane of skin, often covered with fur, that extends from the front limbs, particularly the enormously lengthened ring finger, to the knees or, in some cases, the ankles. This membrane is used for flight, just like the membrane of the (unrelated) bat's wing. To make the animal lighter, the bones, like birds' bones, are filled with air. Just as in most birds, their sight is good and the smell usually poor. Unlike most birds (except the crows and parrots), they are very intelligent and in most cases perfectly trainable. Only the filthy devil *Sordes* sets its mind firmly against personal (or any other) hygiene. It is possible to breed all the smaller pterosaurs, but the smallest long-tailed ones are often obstinate and the largest short-tailed ones can be pretty tricky, too. (As a general rule the short-tailed pterosaurs make better pets than the long-tailed ones: they are brighter, tougher, prettier and, above all, cleaner.)

Because pterosaurs fly, you need to pay particular attention to their housing. *Criorhynchus* and some of the smaller species of *Pterodactylus* can be kept indoors without too much disruption (beware *Sordes*!), but in general plenty of space is needed, as well as access to bodies of water. Shelters should be at least as long and wide as they are high, because pterosaurs do not find it very easy to fly straight upward. There is a danger that they might fall to the floor and be unable to regain their perches. If the shelter is open-fronted, no windows are needed; if it is completely closed in, at least one window (not clear glass, because they will fly into it) should be built into one of the sides to allow in plenty of light. Otherwise, the pterosaurs might not use the shelter and be difficult to drive in at night.

The framework of the outdoor part of the cage can be of sawn timber but rustic poles look much nicer and blend better with the garden surroundings. Sawn timber will have to be painted or creosoted at regular intervals, whereas rustic

Above: A typical Pterosaur coop. Below: Pteradon, *the most beautiful and delicate of the Pterosaurs.*

pair seems to have formed, remove it to a separate breeding enclosure. Here, if you leave the happy couple as undisturbed as you can, they may mate. The cock will display his tail (and in some species his brightly-coloured teeth) and neck-feathers to the hen and sing. This sound, usually raucous, repetitive and unpleasing to our ears, seems to unlock the hen's hitherto pent-up longing: she will then respond, coyly but unmistakeably, to his advances. This response may be brief and temporary to start with: the female may flee if the male progresses too quickly from the oral to the tactile; she may bite persistently irritating cocks. However, as his song stokes up her amatory fire, she will become increasingly receptive to his more palpable approaches, until, eventually, union is consummated. Up to a dozen eggs (thirteen in so-called *A. boulangeria*) are soon laid in a primitive nest in a tree (or shelf, or chandelier). These hatch in three to four weeks, depending on the species. The naked chicks are incubated by the hen until they get their own feathers ten days later. At this stage they are at their most vulnerable: if the hen leaves the nest for too long, the nestlings may catch cold and die. Don't disturb her at this time. Mother and chicks are fed by father. A week or more after fledging, the young are pecking at more or less everything that moves, and can even catch the odd insect. From then on they become more and more self-reliant and independent. If the eggs are soft-shelled, this is probably due to a deficiency of calcium in the mother's diet: next time add lime to her food. However, it may be due to nervous shock: this is usually caused by her partner singing at an inappropriate moment. Try to teach him, by example if you can, that timing is everything.

poles (so I'm told) need no maintenance.

Before we deal in detail with the various species I must issue a warning here. I strongly recommend that you do not attempt to keep *Pteranodon* in captivity. No animal so large and delicate can be kept successfully in captivity. No enclosure can provide them with the conditions they need; attempts to keep them always result in unhappy, unhealthy animals wasting away to an inevitable death. Unlike many pterosaurs, they cannot be released in the hope that they will return to their owner: they float away, never to return.

Enough said: they won't breed in captivity; even if you manage to hatch the eggs yourself, the chicks won't thrive and will scarcely ever reach maturity. Leave them be.

Dinosaur systematists will insist, reasonably enough, that *Archaeopteryx* is a bird. However, it is better, in what is a practical manual, to put it among its close relatives. If you wish to think of it as a bird, do so: both authority and common sense are on your side. Perhaps only snobs and romantics would wish to stress its ancestry in preference to its vulgar relations. Several species are now available; some of these vary a little from the main account.

Most species will pair up naturally if kept in fairly large groups. When such a

Archaeopteryx

'TIME-HONOURED AUGURY', from Greek ἀρχαιος *(ancient, time-honoured) + πτερυξ (augury), from the use of its feathers in fortune-telling by gypsies.*

The first bird! Easily kept, fed and bred, there is an *Archaeopteryx* for every occasion. Choose a species to suit your home and pocket.

One of our smallest dinosaurs, weighing less than 1 kilogram (2 pounds), *Archaeopteryx* looks like a typical, small, long-tailed coelurosaur covered in feathers, like a bird. Like all coelurosaurs, but unlike birds, it has well-developed teeth and grasping hands; like most birds, it has feathers all over its body, and in two rows along its tail. It moults twice a year and in all species the male is more brightly coloured than the drab female. Species differ in colour and pattern; pay your money and take your choice. It can fly, of course.

Treated well, your archy can become quite tame and affectionate and is generally well-behaved in the presence of humans. The squawk of most species is rather like a chair being dragged over a stone floor. If this irritates you, use ear muffs or a Walkman. Its teeth are very sharp, so don't annoy it. In fact, it is a good idea to let it have its own way at all times, and to be as subservient as possible. Get up if it wants to sit in your chair; turn up the heating when it is moulting, even though this will be in mid-summer; ideally, keep a dish of live mice on the coffee table so that it can have a snack whenever it feels like one. Living with *Archaeopteryx* is good for those with over-inflated egos and they therefore make good presents for film stars, talk show hosts, consultant surgeons and government ministers.

Feeding: Different species prefer different foods: in general, try live or recently dead food. Day-old chicks, dragonflies, white mice and cat-food are good, basic stand-bys. Some individuals of at least two species love peanuts, almost to distraction. Juniper berries are usually a great hit, particularly with courting couples, although, if given to ovulating hens, they may cause the eggs to be addled. In the wild, many archies feed on insects, lizards and small mammals. Like most perching birds, it catches its food with its beak. It has many types of feeding behaviour and the food you give a particular species should be related as closely as you can to this behaviour. For example, the Black Archaeopteryx, which has marvellous golden legs,

likes to leap into leaf litter and loose undergrowth, where it scrabbles backwards with its feet (with its arms as well, according to some accounts). This disturbs and reveals the prey, which can then be grabbed by the beak. Give this species the sorts of things you find in undergrowth. Another species, the Melodious Archaeopteryx (song simple but uniquely pleasing) eats molluscs. The Rough-legged Archaeopteryx parachutes from trees onto its prey of shrews and rodents. The Short-eared Archaeopteryx has large eyes and big ears: it is nocturnal and so is its prey, so give it plenty of night-life.

Housing: Although it should live out of doors, it will enjoy being brought into the house from time to time. If you want to see a lot of your pets, build an aviary onto your house so that they can join you in your living quarters whenever they wish. In spite of what many books say, *Archaeopteryx* can fly, though not very strongly and not for long distances. Taking off from a level surface is difficult. Fortunately, the claws on its wings, at the wrist, help it to scramble up trees. Provide it with shrubs and sticks to climb.

Breeding: If you play your cards right, breeding is not only feasible but very likely. The introduction to this chapter will give you some useful hints.

Availability: The finest specimens come from the Archaeopteryx Exchange near Solnhofen in Germany.

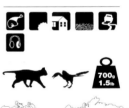

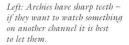

Left: Archies have sharp teeth – if they want to watch something on another channel it is best to let them.

Sordes

'FILTHY', from Latin sordes *(dirt, filth, uncleanness, squalor).*

In Russia *Sordes* is known as 'Hairy Devil' or 'Filthy Feet'! It is, without doubt, a filthy, hairy devil. Perhaps because of this it has undoubted fascination and charm.

Like nearly all pterosaurs, *Sordes* is covered with thick fur, even underneath the wing membrane. The long, prehensile tail is not attached to this membrane, which extends as far as the hind legs. Different species have slightly different coloured fur, but in the most commonly available, *S. pilosus*, the fur is dark reddish-brown.

The nose is sharp and the mouth full of teeth, which are used with some restraint, but not much. The eyes are huge, dark and liquid: it is these that exert that fascination which is later regretted so half-heartedly; for though *Sordes* is a dirty little devil, it is a charming one too. If you find things difficult to forgive, get a little dirty devil and you will discover so much that you need to forgive as well as a new-found ability to do so. Wear protective clothing, including face-mask, when

playing with your hairy devil, and try to keep it out of the house.

Feeding: Although they are carnivores in the wild, in the home they are omnivores. Feeding them is not difficult as such: the problem is their tendency to feed on unwanted organic material and their ingenuity in getting to it. They are messy feeders and totally uninterested in their appearance, so you will have to bath them from time to time. They enjoy this: use a soft scrubbing brush and powerful shampoo (don't let it get in their eyes!). Avoid the temptation to tickle them.

Housing: Give your *Sordes* a draught-proof corner with plenty of branches, horizontal bars or (best) vertical blankets to hang from. Bother less with security than luxury – a proper attitude in many aspects of life – for *Sordes* will stay where it is most comfortable.

Breeding: Their breeding habits are too unspeakable to describe.

Availability: Can be purchased from travelling barrows in Kazakhstan.

Anurognathus

'Frog Face', from Anura (the frogs and toads) + Greek γναθος (jaw).

One of the best-looking of the pterosaurs, *Anurognathus* is ideal for the pond-owner who wants something more original than ornamental waterfowl.

Anurognathus is a very aquatic species in captivity, whose yellow beak and matching hind flippers make it perhaps the most attractive of the pterosaurs. Its fur is a very dark, glossy brown, almost black. It is very fast flying and groups of pterosaur fanciers compete with each other to display their pets' amazing aerobatic skills.

Feeding: Its food is, curiously enough, insects, and you should try to reproduce this diet as exactly as you can in captivity – plenty of dragonflies, mayflies (in season), water boatmen and so on. Lameness and partial paralysis, if they occur, are due to a deficiency of Vitamin D or lime. Crisper insects, such as water beetles, are the answer, but if this fails, try massaging *Anurognathus*'s legs and wings with methylated spirit.

Housing: Water is essential, circulating constantly to prevent its becoming foul. A medium-sized pond of about a hectare (2 ½ acres), netted over at 6 metres (20 feet) or so, should make excellent quarters for a couple of pairs.

Breeding: They pair for life and their marital lives are a model for all of us. Both sexes are beautiful and rather characterless: keep them as ornaments, but don't expect a lot of fun.

Availability: Not easy: try the Archaeopteryx Exchanges in Bavaria.

Criorhynchus

'Mutton Head', from Greek κριος (ram) + ρυγχος (snout).

A lovely pterosaur with a lovely nature. Easily fed, gentle and beautiful, it flourishes luxuriantly in the home and can be treated as one of the family.

This rare and unusual ornithocheirid is my own personal favourite among the pterosaurs. It is unusual in having a wide, keel-like crest at the end of its beak, which gives it a charm shared only by the horrid Hairy Devil, or *Sordes* (see opposite) and, to some extent, *Anurognathus* (see above).

It is gentle and will not harm babies, although the reverse is not always true: make sure you keep all babies away from any household containing *Criorhynchus*.

Feeding: It has only a few teeth, but they are big: what it eats in the wild we don't yet know, but in the home it will eat any fishy food. Some owners claim their *Criorhynchus* eats what and where they do. If you treat your pterosaur as one of the family in this way, it is very important to set a good example to your pet and eat a balanced diet.

Housing: *Criorhynchus* is easily tamed and house-trained: all it needs is a very large parrot-style perch 3 metres (10 feet) above a tray.

Breeding: Captive specimens will not breed, although they flourish. They will court, but that's as far as it goes, even under conditions of extreme privacy: this invariably leads to scarcity in captivity. This coyness may extend to *Criorhynchus*'s behaviour in the wild: if so, it explains the animal's rarity.

Availability: Pterosauros Brasileiras, Santana Formation, Brazil, but unofficial stands at the Archaeopteryx Exchanges in Bavaria may provide you with specimens.

Pterodactylus elegans

'GAY FINGER-WING', from Greek πτερον *(wing)* + δακτυλος *(finger) and Latin* elegans *(luxurious, effeminate).*

This popular and charming handkerchief-sized pterodactyl may be kept in the house. Easily house-trained and happy in the hurly-burly of family life, it is easily fed but not so easily bred.

This is an appealing and tiny pterodactyl, about 15 centimetres (6 inches) long, with small teeth in the front of the jaw. The bull has a golden crown and a blue bib; the cow and calves are much more uniformly coloured but there are usually some greenish streaks on breast and flanks and a buffish stripe over the eye. They love to play hide and seek, preferring to hide rather than seek, and hugely enjoy the surprise aspect of this game. In fact, they frequently hide even when the game has not been suggested, popping out at you and (especially) your visitors, making a low cooing noise, which some wrongly interpret as their way of saying 'boo'. In fact, they make this noise on other occasions – when you trip up, when you spill something, when your car won't start – and it is quite clear that what they are doing is laughing. They are not recommended for the nervous or paranoid.

Feeding: *P. elegans* is an insect eater: in summer it can catch its own food outside, though this may not be feasible in some areas. In other seasons, mealworms and gentles are a good basic diet. Experiment with other types of food: try small biscuits, vitamin capsules (especially D), tarantula scratchings and liver shreds.

Housing: *P. elegans* is sociable to the point of gregariousness and should be kept in small herds of twenty or more. Alternatively, single specimens, especially bulls, may be kept in the house, rather like a cat or bantam. Give them as large a cage as you can manage, with plenty of perches, and allow them the run of the house as often as possible. They are easily, but not quickly, house-trained and are happiest in the confusion of family life; the presence of children is particularly valuable to absorb some of the animal high spirits usually shown by healthy and affectionate bulls.

Breeding: Difficult to breed owing to rampant homosexuality.

Availability: Good specimens available from the Solnhofen Archaeopteryx Exchange in Germany.

Dsungaripterus

'Wing from Jungarr', from Dsungar(in Xinjiang province) + Greek πτερον (wing).

A highly recommended species. A calf hand-reared from the egg becomes very tame. It will live happily in a garden that has a pond, and at night is happy to hang up in the gutter.

In *Dsungaripterus* the teeth have been lost from the front part of the jaws, which are used to winkle shellfish out of crannies on the shore or to prize them off rocks. The underside is white and the back grey, indicating that is does a bit of fishing on the side.

Dsungaripterus is an intelligent animal that can be trained by rewarding it with food. It is worth training it to spear intruders while it is hanging on the roof of your house at night. Be careful to teach it to distinguish between bona fide visitors and the unwelcome. Tell your friends to whistle a well-known tune, like 'My Way', 'I Do Like to Be Beside the Seaside' or John Cage's '4'33''' (tacet), as they approach your house, and reward *Dsungaripterus* when it does not attack them. A useful side-effect is that insurance salesmen, children who have kicked balls into your garden and worthy people collecting for charity quickly learn not to bother you. You can try to protect such people by putting up a large notice: 'Cave Dsungaripterus', but some of them may not know what it means and those that do will almost certainly dismiss it as a joke.

During the day it is usually as sweet as pie, and does not normally show any aggression. Even when it is being a little bit of a nuisance at picnics by begging for food with its curious vulture-like song, or poking its beak into your lap to obtain pieces of food that have dropped there, its personality exudes wholesome bonhomie. It wants to be one of the lads and do what you are doing. (It should go without saying that you should be very circumspect in its presence: it will imitate your every action if it can.)

Feeding: Its back teeth are broad and flattened, and are good at crushing food. It loves to eat shellfish: oysters and limpets are its favourites, but most specimens are happy to eat anything fishy you have, particularly if it's crunchy. Crabs, lobsters and baby terrapins are a real godsend. If feeding becomes a problem, place a regular wholesale order with your fishmonger.

Housing: Because of its size and fishy diet, *Dsungaripterus* is best kept in a very large outdoor aviary enclosing a lake, but it is very accommodating about its accommodation. A calf raised from the egg will become extremely tame and loathe to leave what it considers its home. Although too big to allow inside any but the stateliest homes, it will happily live in a garden, as long as there is a largish pond in it. At night it likes to hang itself up by its toes from the roof or gutter, where it is troubled only by the fiercest weather. Although wide, *Dsungaripterus* is light and delicate: in windy weather it may become entangled in branches, wires and so on. All the larger pterosaurs have trouble with wind and should be brought indoors when the Beaufort Scale exceeds 4. If chronic wind is part of your environment, as in the Falkland Islands, and there is no chance of flight outside, provide a large aircraft hangar with a pond in it and ledges for the pterosaur to depend on. Usually, like Southern judges, *Dsungaripterus* will cope with bluster and carry on hanging.

Breeding: Breeding is fairly regular, producing two elliptical eggs. Some individuals seem ignorant of proper incubation procedures. In these cases, it is best to remove the eggs and incubate them yourself. Airing cupboards are often recommended but not by those who've tried them. As with so many things, having them in bed with you at night and under an electric blanket (set to high) in the daytime is still the best bet for *Dsungaripterus* eggs.

Availability: Markets in Sinkiang province, China.

10kg
22lb

4 | DINOSAURS FOR RECREATION AND THE CIRCUS

In a way this chapter is superfluous: nearly all dinosaurs may be used for recreation; the three I have chosen are just the ones that are most commonly used or, rather, the ones that were most commonly used twenty years ago, when the first edition of this book was published. Since then things have changed a great deal, particularly in the world of the circus. Animals of all kinds are being banished from the world of mass entertainment, so the spectacular acts of the past, such as the *Postosuchus*-training, the bare back *Kentrosaurus*-riding, the placing of the head into the *Dromaeosaurus's* mouth and the brontosaur tightrope walk, have had to be sacrificed at the altar of political correctness.

But all is not lost: domestic entertainment and recreation remain, and dinosaurs are increasingly being employed in groups and teams for activities that used to be for humans, horses and dogs only.

I have to say straight away that I thoroughly disapprove of the use of dromaeosaurs for 'bull-fighting', an extreme sport that has spread from parts of Iberia to some of the newer members of the European Community. Quite apart from the ethical problems that always seem to crop up in activities leading to inevitable human death, dromaeosaur-fighting and its cheaper daughter, dromaeosaur-baiting, lack the unpredictability needed for an exciting spectator sport. So far, no dromaeosaur has been killed and no dromeador has survived: a success rate of 0% does not guarantee a full house. Bare-knuckle boxing with ankylosaurs has also had a predictably rocky start. Sporting dinosaur owners must get real.

Get real in what way? The answer lies in traditional activities. Holiday camps and bathing beaches are ideal venues for dinosaur delights, but you must keep the more inquisitive animals (compies are a particular nuisance) away from barbecues and fireworks. Activities such as hunting *Bambiraptor* (where permitted), golf (caddying only) and tobogganing (with or without toboggan) have proved very popular, with particularly talented animals fetching enormous prices and prizes. And this is the point: it all depends on your dinosaur. All these activities need to be tailored to the individual that shows talent. There's no point in taking a *Velociraptor* to the club or dance hall if it doesn't dance in time: even the conga requires rhythm. But if your beast has talent, it's a different story. You will have noticed the improvement in organization at Wimbledon since ball-dinosaurs were introduced; dino-caddies are now accepted in golf (although in the American Masters only males have been used so far); even sports such as cricket and baseball are using the more accomplished club-tailed ankylosaurs to entertain the crowds between innings with displays of power-hitting.

Ancient sports such as falconry have received a real shot in the arm with the introduction of pterosaurs; you need look no further than the foreword of this book (although I hope you will) to see how little the techniques have changed since the time of King Sargon II of Assyria: even the language has that eastern incomprehensibility embraced by all blood sports. In addition to the species I have recommended, which are really intended for domestic use and pleasure (although there has been a great deal of success with *Dsungaripterus*), potential falconers should consider other pterosaurs such as *Ornithocheirus* and the larger species of *Pterodactylus*. By the way, some falconers have even succeeded with *Tapejara*, with squid threatening to overtake more conventional prey in many coastal areas. There has been less interest in carrion: flying at road-kills has yet to take off, although this type of hawking might be thought to be of particular interest to the older pterosaur-owner.

Perhaps it would not be out of place here to deal with the absence of any recommendation for *Bambiraptor* in this book. This attractive little dino has been adored by thousands of schoolchildren for its fluffy body, loving nature and ability to look after itself. But in the wild it is a pest, killing game-birds like pheasant and grouse and game-fish like salmon and trout; worse than this, it also kills deer and duck, apparently taking pleasure in the chase. No wonder the first of my recommended dinosaurs, *Ornithomimus*, is now proving so useful in the hunting field.

What about my other two recommendations, *Gallimimus* and *Dromaeosaurus*? *Gallimimus* has been particularly hard hit by the demise of animal acts in circuses, where it specialized in acts of daring and stoicism. This stoicism, together with good eye-sight, has made it ideal for umpiring cricket matches, particularly test matches, which may last for five days without any appreciable action. Off the sports field, other talents of *Gallimimus* can be exploited. Nowhere is this more evident than on the dance floor. Any dance involving high kicks is improved tenfold by the addition of a troupe of these glamorous dinosaurs. The less talented may content themselves with morris dancing, but the Gorgeous Gallimimids of the Galop have made the Pigalle in Paris a byword for Gallic insouciance and chic.

Which leaves us with *Dromaeosaurus*. In this dinosaur we have a creature of extremes. If it is intelligent and well-trained, it can do nearly anything; if it is an individual that has been badly trained, or an individual that is not that brainy, then problems can occur. We find the best holding down posts in casinos and night clubs (usually at the door), at pop-festivals and in sports centres. They are valuable assistants to personal trainers, being very helpful in motivating otherwise unwilling clients.

To summarize: most types of dinosaur can be used for recreation purposes, but not all individuals are suitable. If you choose one of the following three, you will have a head's start on your competitors, always useful in your dealings with dinosaurs.

Ornithomimus

'Bird Mime-artist', from Greek ορνιθικος *(bird-like)* + μιμος *(a mimic or actor), because it looks like a bird and acts like one.*

An appealing first dinosaur for the child anxious for her first ride. Easy to break in, tractable and undemanding to feed. Conveniently housed in your paddock.

If you want to keep something more exciting than the usual coelurosaur, *Ornithomimus* is an ideal beginner's choice. As well as long, thin avian legs, it has a tiny head, a bird-like beak, seldom any teeth and a long tail stiffened as a counterbalance to the long neck. The larger specimens, at nearly 4 metres (13 feet) long, are a little awkward and yet very amenable to captivity. They have no claws that catch and they don't bite; they rely on speed to avoid their enemies and their legs, like Helena's, are longer to run away. For a dinosaur, *Ornithomimus* has a larger than average brain, although it is still no genius. However, a tamed individual is gentle and easily trained and can be ridden with saddle and bridle. A grumpy one can annihilate a child with a kick, so (on most occasions) a gentle specimen is recommended. The smaller species, 2–3 metres (7–10 feet) long, can be kept in a paddock and broken in for children; the larger ones are very exciting to ride.

Learning to ride *Ornithomimus* is more like learning to ride a bicycle than a horse: you have to believe in your combined ability to stand up. Once you have achieved this, you find that the creature's walk is secure and sedate; unfortunately, this gives many novice riders an unwarranted sense of confidence, which may prompt them to try trotting. The trot is best described as a rhythmic earthquake: the animal lurches from side to side as the weight is jerkily transferred from one foot to the other and the unpractised rider is shaken almost senseless as she (or he) desperately struggles to slow her (or his) dinosaur back to a walk.

It is best to leave trotting to those who have made a hobby, and sometimes a profession, out of *Ornithomimus* dressage. The beginner should walk the animal on roads and move it swiftly to a canter and then a gallop when he (or she) reaches grass. The cantering *Ornithomimus* is another curious spectacle. The animal keeps its legs straight and skips,

and the rider finds that her (or his) body above the waist takes on a rhythmical twisting motion – one shoulder forward then the other – rather like someone drying his (or her) back in slow motion. This is not as painful as trotting, but it is very inelegant. Move up to a gallop as soon as you can, for a galloping *Ornithomimus* simply runs with its head stretched forward; the upper part of its body becomes stable and the rider at last feels comfortable and able to acknowledge the cheers of her (or his) friends. Under the Big Top, in the ring, nothing stimulates a bareback rider more than an *Ornithomimus*.

Feeding: *Ornithomimus* is one of the easiest dinosaurs to feed and it will eat all brands of cat- and dog-food as well as most scraps from the table. Like the ostrich, it is a gastronomic polymath. Feed it a stoat, or some other kind of small mammal, as an occasional treat.

Housing: As a horse, but keep it warmer in winter.

Breeding: This is the only dinosaur genus in which copulation occurs after egg-laying and before hatching. *Ornithomimus* can be bred without difficulty. At seven weeks or so the mother relaxes and the young can be removed from her care. Such home-hatched chicks are ideal for training.

Availability: The Montana DinoMart, the Colorado Dinosaur Depot and the Lhasa Bazaars. Red Deer River Retailers of Alberta seem to have lost some of their edge.

Left: Ornithomimus *is a delight to ride – as long as you can avoid trotting.*

Gallimimus

'Cock Mimic', from Latin gallus *(cock)* + mimus *(mimic).*

An ideal ornithomimid for beginners, as well as holding great appeal to circus proprietors; can be house-trained and is good with children, as well as being unusually easily fed.

This ornithomimid, as its name suggests, is chicken-like in appearance, with a long neck, and is about 4 metres (13 feet) long. Some chicken! Some neck! *Gallimimus* is ideal for the novice ornithomimid-keeper: it can even be house-trained, in all senses of the word, and is gentle enough not to worry children, although babies are a temptation. Its greatest qualities are its keenness to please and its boundless sense of fun. It can be trained to perform acts of daring, such as jumping through hoops of fire and walking the tightrope, as well as acts of straightforward stoicism, such as standing still while custard pies are pushed into its face. In the home, or better still, the garden, *Gallimimus* will willingly take part in games of football or hockey, where it is happy to act as a goalpost for hours on end; if you like, it will wade in your lake pulling your boat. In Argentina it is now used as a pony in polo; in Paraguay it is still used as a goal.

Feeding: Unlike a chicken, *Gallimimus* must have a mainly meaty diet. It abominates biscuits.

Housing: As *Ornithomimus* (see p. 39).

Breeding: They are difficult to breed, but success has been achieved in Chettle, Dorset and in Virginia. If you want to have a go, try raising the temperature to 30°C (86°F) or more, and sprinkling both sexes (at the same time) with warm water. A plastic cage within a well-heated bathroom makes an ideal love-nest, and *Gallimimus* will enjoy it too. Always keep it warm and provide your pet with plenty of toys and playmates. If you are lucky, you will see their famous courtship display, in which both cock and hen march together side by side, inflate their brightly coloured throat patches and perform their highly individual courtship song. This wonderful duet was copied, almost note for note, by Wolfgang A. Mozart, and used as the love duet between Papageno and Papagena ('Pa-pa-gena!' ... 'Pa-pa-geno!') in his opera *The Magic Flute*. In fact, most professional breeders always make sure that the *Gallimimus* love-nest is provided with a suitable sound system and CDs of the opera. Bring them into the mood with 'Der Vogelfänger bin ich ja'; cool them down if the action gets too rough too soon with 'Hm! hm! hm! hm!'; and if the cock seems discouraged, try 'Ich Narr! Vergaß der Zauberdinger!'.

Availability: The horse markets in Ulan Bator, Mongolia, often have a few spare specimens at the end of the season.

Dromaeosaurus

'DROMIO LIZARD' from Dromio, the twin slaves in Shakespeare's
Comedy of Errors + *Greek* σαυρος *(lizard)*.

An interesting and uncompromising dinosaur, probably suitable for the domestic owner but an exciting challenge for the Big Top.

This vivacious little native of Late Cretaceous Canada is essentially a smaller version of *Deinonychus* and (contrary to my previous recommendation) suitable for the intrepid private collector, who will enjoy teaching it tricks. It is intelligent but fierce, entertaining but dangerous. Plate armour should be worn, as chain mail bruises the wearer and damages the dinosaur's toes. Japanese and other Oriental armour is not robust enough, often leading to a lack of confidence in the wearer. I recommend pinioning it before public display (see *Deinonychus*, p. 51).

The toreador will be stimulated by the challenge of matching his skills against the trenchant teeth, grasping hands and sharp claws of this dextrous and intelligent killing machine, even if it is likely to be the last time. Lion tamers, a dying breed, will also

want to try their hands in the circus. And not only their hands: in the first edition of this book I said that the first person who can put his head into the jaws of *Dromaeosaurus* while wearing a sequinned leotard will shoot to stardom. This prophecy still stands.

What of its softer side? *Dromaeosaurus* as company for the lonely, solace to the celibate, friend of the forlorn? There are dangers, of course: *Dromaeosaurus* as a personal pal is no pushover, and a false step on your part may be your last. But for many friendless people the prospect of a swift and sudden dis-embowelling is a small price to pay for what may prove to be an almost mystical unity of mind and spirit. Or, at the very least, an occasional companion.

Feeding: As *Velociraptor* (see p. 46).
Housing: As *Velociraptor* (see p. 46).
Breeding: As *Velociraptor* (see p. 46).
Availability: The Red Deer River Retailers, Alberta.

5 | DINOSAURS FOR SECURITY WORK

Many of the security-linked tasks now allocated to dogs, horses and men could be done better by dinosaurs. Police work is an obvious example, but crowd control at football matches and rock concerts, night club bouncing, bodyguards for potentates and escorting school outings also leap to mind, although some careful thought should be given to the last. Guard-dinos are becoming poular too. Let us look at these in turn.

Police work

Many police forces in Britain now use dinosaurs for beat work, particularly in inner-city areas. *Coelophysis* and *Ornitholestes* are the most popular: *Ornitholestes*, being smaller than *Coelophysis*, is usually the dino of choice for female police officers, even though it is, if anything, even less inclined to compromise than *Coelophysis*. Both species need months of training with their minder, and neither of them is inclined to obey anyone else. It goes without saying that these are not ideal dinosaurs for the private owner, although too often they are used to guard the more ostentatious properties. They are popular with pop stars, to start with at least. Both these species are used to police demonstrations, although groups of *Velociraptor* are often preferred when trouble is anticipated.

Crowd control

As I have said elsewhere, dinosaurs, though in many ways absolutely ideal for keeping crowds under control at sporting occasions such as football matches, or at rock concerts, have sometimes caused more problems than they have solved. This has been in most cases due to shortcomings of the handlers, who have often tried to control crowds before having learnt to control dinosaurs. No *Ornitholestes*, be it never so gentle, will pass up the opportunity of a providential snack unless it has been very thoroughly trained. Until a satisfactory licensing scheme is decided upon and properly enforced, the only people who should be allowed to use the more rigorous species for crowd control are professionals (at present, this means the police) and bouncers. Bouncing, the technique used to control entry into clubs and other similar establishments, is not yet classed as a profession (some people argue that the academic content and intellectual rigour of the thirty-minute course are not sufficient to justify the award of formal qualifications) but works very well within a local authority licensing scheme. There have been very few problems outside night clubs since dinosaurs, particularly *Ornitholestes*, have become a familiar feature at their entrances. This is because dinosaur-handlers at clubs, whether or not they have a criminal record, and whether or not they have a history of drug dealing or grievous bodily harm, are required by the local authority to be proficient in handling dinosaurs 'for the purposes of personnel control within confined spaces' and to 'hold or display or show to an authorized officer of the council or licensing or authorizing authority a dinosaur-handling licence as authorized by the council or licensing or authorizing authority or to indicate to the said authorized officer where such licence or other authorization approved by the licensing or authorizing authority may be seen by the aforesaid authorizing authority' (*Dinosaur-authorizing Authorizing Authority Handbook*)!

Bodyguards

People who consider themselves at risk of violence sometimes use dinosaurs for personal protection. Many of them can be trained to act as personal minders. *Oviraptor* and *Troodon* are best for this. *Velociraptor* is best in packs, although you can sometimes persuade a female to leave her group and commit herself totally to your welfare: such a jewel is beyond price. *Ornitholestes* is very effective, of course, but too often oversteps the mark.

Escorting school outings

The chronic underfunding of schools has tempted some headteachers to cut corners in the education of children. Alarm bells should have rung when some inner-city schools started using dinosaurs to supervise classes during the absence of the form teachers. On the positive side, headteachers could point to the definite improvement in the teacher/pupil ratio; on the negative side, lawyers' fees had an adverse effect on school budgets. Although the jury is still out on this one, it is generally agreed that the experiment of using dinosaurs to escort childrens' outings to museums, art galleries and games matches was not thought through carefully enough.

Guard-dinos

If you wish to protect your property rather than your person, you may use any of the dinosaurs in this section to discourage intruders. In fact, even quite small ones may be useful: half a dozen compies snapping at a burglar's heels, or higher, will deter the impulse thief; a single strategically placed *Triceratops* will divert the attention even of skilled professionals. *Therizinosaurus*, although gentle enough with those it knows, is likely to turn nasty when it spots a stranger. All these have their place as domestic guards, but I should like to suggest that you give one of the larger pterosaurs a try: I recommend *Dsungaripterus*. Indeed, the more forward-looking insurance companies will offer discounts on the premiums of those householders who keep free-range pterosaurs on their land, particularly if they (the pterosaurs) have undergone the short intruder recognition courses that many local authorities now provide, not only for pterosaurs but also for dinosaurs. At a typical course your pet will be taught A) to spot the intruder (is it a man, rather than, say, a fox or tumbleweed?), B) to identify the intruder (is it a friend of the family, rather than a stranger?) and C) to act appropriately. Many of the courses are very effective, although some difficulties have yet to be overcome. For example, while 'spotting intruders' is taught easily enough, 'identifying intruders' is more of a problem. Some late-night visitors are very welcome to the resident, even though they may not be familiar to all members of the family, or to the pterosaur. Some courses are experimenting with a system of identity-beacons, which produce either a series of coded light signals or else an auditory cypher, which can be recognized by the trainee animal. 'Acting appropriately' is usually straight-forward enough, though commonly the intruder provokes behaviour patterns that do not really fit the occasion. Many a burglar has fled from the scene of his intended crime to the shelter of a local police station in order to escape the attentions of an amorous pterosaur. But the result is the same: the owner can sleep happy in the knowledge that his home is safe from the thief in the night.

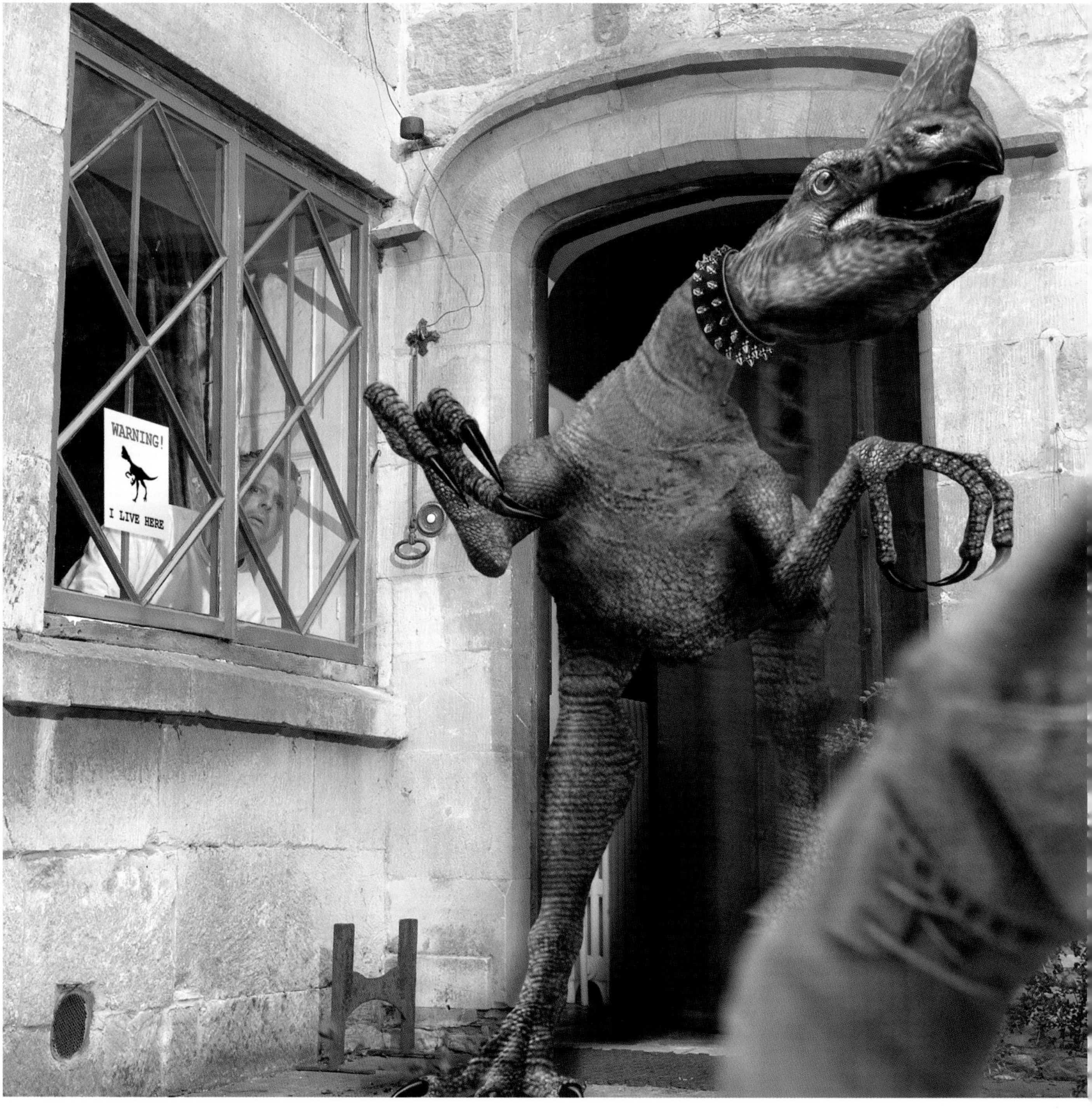
WARNING!
I LIVE HERE

Oviraptor

'TRIUMPHANT CATCHER', from Latin ovans *(triumphing in ovation)* + raptor *(one who seizes and carries off), from the apparent pleasure with which it apprehends malefactors.*

A charming coelurosaur, easily fed. Although it is difficult to train, you can collar it and exercise it on a chain. Useful as a guard on your premises.

This lightly built dinosaur is about 2 metres (6 ½ feet) long, half of which is tail. It is quite like a wallaby in shape, with large hind legs and smaller front legs. Unlike a wallaby, it walks and runs on its hind legs without the help of a tail or front legs. It leaps upon strangers, biting and squealing with delight: this can be of great use to security organizations and to guard the home, but make sure your own pet knows who your friends are or you may lose them, perhaps permanently. If you can persuade your specimen to wear a collar, you can exercise it outside, in street or park, just as you would exercise a wallaby, although you will need to be careful in the vicinity of kindergartens and primary schools. Because it is so fond of eggs, you will need to take extra precautions if you live anywhere near a poultry farm. *Oviraptor* is quite capable of eating a hundred eggs at a sitting, preferring this to the effort of eating their mothers. It will also have a go at any oval or round object: it never seems to learn that footballs are not nice to eat.

Feeding: Although it is carnivorous, *Oviraptor* is in many ways ideal for the beginner. It will eat most recognized dog-foods, meaty scraps of various sorts, and eggs, particularly those of ceratopids.

Housing: They can only be allowed in the house under supervision. However, if you keep it on a running leash in your garden, it will bark – or rather squeal – at intruders and jump on them if they come near; this is usually enough to deter all but the most enthusiastic burglars.

Breeding: Easily bred. Give it a sand-pit, and, after mating, the female will make a mound, scoop out a hollow and lay up to twenty eggs in it; both sexes incubate the clutch. Do not try to take the eggs, as both sexes will guard the nest fiercely.

Availability: The usual Mongolian outlets.

Left: Oviraptor *delights in greeting doorstep salesmen.*

Velociraptor

'FLEET RAVISHER', from Latin velox, velocis *(fleet)*
+ raptor *(one who seizes by force).*

A splendid, loyal, fierce friend. For the country sportsman who wants real sport or for the police force that needs to get its man.

Unfortunately, the film *Jurassic Park* and its less worthy children have sown confusion in the public mind by confusing *Velociraptor* with *Deinonychus*, its big cousin. *Velociraptor*, including its long tail, is seldom more than 2 metres (6 ½ feet) long, less than half the size of *Deinonychus*, which is so well portrayed, but misnamed *Velociraptor*, in Spielberg's excellent movie.

It is, at its best, a splendid, loyal creature. It can be fierce, it's true, and some individuals, particularly the cocks, seem untameable. They can inflict severe wounds with their hind claws, just as *Deinonychus* can, and strange children should not be encouraged to stroke them. But the right animal in the right hands is a marvellous combination. Tame dinosaurs may be taken for runs in the country, where they will catch their own prey, particularly if they are allowed to hunt in flocks. They should be kept clear of sheep, goats, calves, pigs and small people, as they are accomplished rapists.

They have been scandalously underutilized in security work, although popular in the navy.

Feeding: The real *Velociraptor* is a small but agile carnivore with slender legs and long, clutching hands. It is very much a flesh-eater, needing meat in large quantities (some specimens, it is true, can be weaned on to corned beef but this is not really economical). It is intelligent and will respond to rigorous training.

Housing: As a lion.

Breeding: Easy to breed if kept unsupervised in large, secure enclosures.

Availability: The raptor markets of Mongolia and China.

Ornitholestes

'Bird Robber', from Greek ὄρνιθος *(bird)* + ληστής *(robber), from its tendency to break into poultry farms.*

Perhaps less suitable than *Coelophysis* for domestic use but suitable for the apprehension of suspected malefactors. Would suit rural police force.

Ornitholestes will make you think of *Coelophysis* (see p. 48), but, although it is not as long, it is a slightly more formidable carnivore, probably best kept out of the home. Like *Coelophysis*, it has long, thin legs, and arms with grasping fingers, balanced by a long, stiff tail. In spite of its height, it is unexpectedly light, as its bones are filled with air.

It can be fairly tractable if brought up from the egg; indeed, many individuals, even those obtained as adults, adapt easily to the conditions of captivity, particularly (it must be said) cocks. The hen is more difficult, although once she has adapted herself she makes a more satisfactory captive than he does. Both sexes are real scamps and it is difficult to be angry with them for long, although dog-owners and parents can be a real trial at times if you have a healthy and active *Ornitholestes*. What a pity so few people seem to have a sense of humour!

Ornitholestes can be trained for the same tasks as *Coelophysis*, although you must take even more care to prevent it maiming its captives. The same sorts of conditions should be provided. It is not as easy to catch as *Coelophysis*, but the reverse is not true: it is even less safe with small children than *Coelophysis* is.

Specimens advertised as *Coelurus* are indistinguishable from *Ornitholestes*.

Feeding: *Ornitholestes* is an active hunter in the wild (the forests and swamps of Late Jurassic Wyoming) and catches small reptiles and mammals, or the young of other dinosaurs. It is a scavenger, too, occupying to some extent the ecological niche filled in Quaternary Kenya by hyenas and jackals. Feeding is, therefore, no problem: as much offal as it can eat, twice a week, keeps it healthy and happy.

Housing: As *Velociraptor* (see opposite).

Breeding: As *Velociraptor* (see opposite).

Availability: Many Olde Worlde Dino Shoppynge Centers in Wyoming, U.S.A. provide *Ornitholestes*, but Bone Cabin Quarry near Como is the best.

13kg
29lb

Coelophysis

'WELSHMAN', from Greek κοιλος *(lying in a valley) +* φυσιος *(sex).*

Fast, agile and inquisitive, an entertaining and easily fed coelurosaur. A perfect dinosaur for catching people, but easily tamed and suitable for a young childless couple.

This is a typical coelurosaur and very slender: its métier is agility. Its long, thin neck ends in a small head with jaws full of tiny saw-edged teeth. It has a long, thin tail to balance its long, thin neck, and long, thin back legs which it runs on. On its forelegs it has hands with three long, thin fingers. The biggest *Coelophysis* is about 3 metres (10 feet) long from tip of nose to tip of tail, but it weighs less than 20 kilograms (44 pounds).

Coelophysis is very inquisitive and its long, grasping hands can be used to snatch small lap-dogs, for instance, which are then hurried away to be eaten at leisure. It is a bit of a nuisance in this way, but, with proper precautions, it will become a merry pet, as long as you don't have any other small animals or children.

Coelophysis won't attack anything larger than a medium-sized dog or three-year-old child (unless trained to) and it is intelligent. It can be taught to perform useful tasks in any situation where there are no small, living animals. For example, tennis-players find that *Coelophysis* make excellent ballboys, and they can also be trained to play triads on the piano with their three fingers. Jazz pianists prepared to persevere find it convenient to have *Coelophysis* playing rhythmical right-hand parts so that they can concentrate on developing chord sequences in the left hand.

However, the greatest potential of *Coelophysis* is as an aid to overstretched police and intelligence services, as they can run faster than any human and can be trained to obey commands. A top *Coelophysis* working with a skilled handler will apprehend, but not kill, even in the most extreme circumstances. It revels in its speed and ability to dodge machine-gun fire, missiles and little-known oriental weapons.

Feeding: Although it is carnivorous, *Coelophysis* will happily settle for all sorts of vaguely meaty food. It seems to eat almost anything given to it, as long as it is not too obviously vegetable: eggs, fish, cat-food, dog-food, parrot-food, muesli, corned beef and so on. It rejects curry. Most dinosaurs, and *Coelophysis* is no exception, like such green leaves as rocket, chickweed, dandelion and viper's bugloss from time to time and especially during the breeding season. It thrives on meat and two vegetables.

Housing: *Coelophysis* is an entertaining dinosaur and because it is so fast and agile you will need to provide plenty of space and good fencing, preferably inturned at the top to prevent the animal climbing out.

Breeding: *Coelophysis* will breed readily, in normal coelurosaur fashion, but is prone to cannibalism.

Availability: The Coelurosaur Trading Center in Connecticut is the best New England source, while Ghost Ranch Theropods in Abiquiu, New Mexico serves the South and the West Coast.

Troodon

*'GIFT-TRAMPLER', from Old Norse troo (trampling) + Greek δωρον (gift),
after its sometimes clumsy treatment of stolen presents.*

Perhaps the most rewarding of the saurornithoidids; small, agile, bipedal and
immensely intelligent. As a guard or friend it can scarcely be bettered, being
loyal and easily trained.

Although *Troodon* is bigger than most birds, it has a very bird-like appearance. It has an intelligent look about it, a genuine desire to please and the ability to perform really useful tasks. It is small and agile (for a dinosaur), and is entirely bipedal and therefore chic. It has slender legs and long, clutching hands, often used to steal small items left in the home.

Chained in your back garden, it will alert you to intruders, but it is more imaginative to teach it, at the ring of a bell, to put out plates and cups, squeeze oranges, grind coffee, remove the lids from yogurt cartons and make toast. Give it a hug and let it sit with you at the table whenever it achieves this satisfactorily. The really brilliant ones will also run baths, switch on electric blankets and put out dustbins, as well as keep the garden clear of unwanted domestic animals.

If you obtain one young, either a cock or a hen will prove responsive, though it may display its gentle side only to its owner. Most specimens do not quite reach 3 metres (10 feet) in length, and half of this is tail, so it is relatively manageable, although looking after it can be a bit Sisyphean. You should always keep it on a leash when it is not in its stout cage: its long hands are quite capable of snatching dogs and other passing animals, which then disappear quickly. You must also keep *Troodon* clear of prams outside shops, even when it is on a leash. If you manage to avoid problems caused by pet-owners and parents, the great intelligence of this little dinosaur makes it an excellent and rewarding companion.

Feeding: Like the other deinonychosaurs, *Troodon* is carnivorous and needs plenty of good, red meat.

Housing: As *Velociraptor* (see p. 46).

Breeding: As *Velociraptor*, but much easier.

Availability: Steveville Stenonychostore and Red Deer River Retailers in Alberta often have specimens available.

Deinonychus

'Terrible Claw', from Greek δεινός (terrible) + όνυξ (claw).

For the careful and socially responsible owner an entire flock is most fulfilling. For a government seeking an unconventional weapon this species could be the answer.

A typical deinonychosaur, *Deinonychus* is about a metre (3 feet) high. It is a carnivore, with powerful teeth and jaws, and its arms are long and gangling with three long-clawed fingers on each hand. The hind legs are what you have to watch: it walks upon two of the claws but holds the third one up off the ground, facing forward. This third claw is 12 centimetres (5 inches) long, razor sharp and sickle-shaped. It can be swung through 180 degrees to project downwards and backwards, and is used to disembowel prey, which is held at arm's length by the forearms. The long tail is rigid and horizontal: it acts as a balancing pole.

There is a major problem: the third claw. This is designed for eviscerating, and human victims are not uncommon: one angry swipe is enough and no amount of dromaeosaurid regret (and they are often heart-rendingly penitent) can bring the victim back to life. At last regulations are being drawn up to compel all private owners to trim the third claw. (A small operation, similar to pinioning in wildfowl, is now carried out, at some expense, to remove the last finger-joint. The animal is unimpaired in its movement and no longer lethal.) *Deinonychus* rarely bites in anger.

As *Deinonychus* was discovered only in 1969 there has been little opportunity to see how it can be useful to its owner. However, it is an extremely intelligent dinosaur and a handful of advanced owners who have been through the other intelligent species – *Gallimimus*, *Dsungaripterus*, *Troodon*, to name only three – have managed to tame *Deinonychus* and then train it and test its intelligence. There are several *Deinonychus* who can play Poker and are brought together by their owners to play in tournaments against each other. The dinosaurs play in groups of four, sitting at small tables. However, it is clear that the dinosaur's greatest potential is military: it has been used successfully in many special operations against terrorists and in the interrogation of prisoners. It is unfortunate that on the two

occasions that it was used in crowd control (a football match and an anti-hunting demonstration) the animals were poorly supervised: the experiment has now been abandoned.

Feeding: *Deinonychus* is exclusively carnivorous and likes its food in great, bleeding chunks: you will need a regular order with your butcher. If you can, give it piglets or lambs: throw them into the enclosure and look away. For snacks, pigeons and guinea pigs are much appreciated. *Deinonychus* will not eat mice or other small mammals, nor can it be trained to take dog-foods (although dogs are another matter: does your neighbour have an irritating rottweiler?). Add to this the fact that *Deinonychus* does not like to be alone (it flourishes only if kept in groups of five), and it becomes clear that you cannot keep this dinosaur on the cheap.

Housing: As *Velociraptor* (see p. 46).
Breeding: As *Velociraptor* (see p. 46).
Availability: Montana DinoMart.

Left: Deinonychus *will only play Poker for high steaks.*

6 | DINOSAURS FOR EGGS AND MEAT

If you have been devastated by Foot and Mouth or Fowl Pest, you have an opportunity, with the assistance of astutely chosen dinosaurs, to recover your assets. If you have been badgered by bovine tuberculosis, you may cast your worries aside and let your new, large-scale flocks safely graze. If your yields have been smaller because of foxes, you may cast aside your pink coats and horns, secure in the knowledge that your dinosaurs will cock snooks at any local predators. The imaginative farmer will diversify into tourism, with his stock attracting profitable sightseers as well as providing both a steady deluge of eggs and occasional bonanzas of meat. Some species may be hired to neighbours for scrub-clearance, heavy haulage and any other tasks that are appropriate to their scale and docility.

For the benefit of farmers looking to continue with meat production, let us look at a typical example of a good meat-dino to start with: *Plateosaurus* (always keeping in mind that much of this account is also true of the other dinosaurs I recommend). *Plateosaurus* will undoubtedly become economically important, because it is easily kept in fairly large numbers under relatively intense conditions, although the European Commission is looking into a minority of abuse cases. Although the market for dinosaur meat is still small, it is growing

steadily and there is no doubt that large quantities of meat can be provided by these dinosaurs for little running cost. For the imaginative farmer, *Plateosaurus* is ideal, because a female is usually only about 6 metres (20 feet) long and a small flock can be kept in a traditional cattle farm with minimal modifications.

The meat has a pleasant flavour, rather like crocodile and *Camptosaurus*, but tougher and therefore less suitable for dinoburgers. It is best either well roasted or well stewed. Cuts from the sirloin are extremely popular and should be roasted at a low heat, allowing about thirty minutes per kilo: baste regularly and sprinkle with rosemary or thyme.

Males are bigger than females in most herbivorous dinosaurs and it has been suggested that they could be castrated like male beef cattle. This, so the argument goes, would remove their aggressiveness and, by making them fatter, would cause more forage to be converted into saleable meat. Unfortunately, the castration of dinosaurs is not as easy as it sounds: the testes are internal and their removal would entail an operation that requires greater surgical skill than the traditional two sharp bricks.

Hadrosaurs

Although *Plateosaurus* is a good starting point, the serious, large-scale dinosaur farmer will soon move on to the hadrosaurs, or duck-bills, a really fine group of dinosaurs. There are more than thirty species of hadrosaurs and with them we move closer to the layman's, or B-movie-style, dinosaur (although there is a long way to go yet). There is often a crest down the centre of the back and the stiff tail. The neck is mobile; the skin is covered with a mosaic of small scales or nodules and is often strikingly patterned. Some species are flat-headed, some have solid crests and some have hollow crests.

Perhaps the hadrosaur's least characteristic feature is the one that gives it its familiar name: duck-billed dinosaur. It does have a rounded upper jaw with a flat tip bearing a horny beak, which it uses to crop foliage, but in the living hadrosaur this beak is usually hidden by the muscles of the face and jaws: it doesn't look at all duck-billed. I am tempted to believe that the man (or woman) who gave them their popular name had never seen one alive. Hadrosaurs are on average 10 metres (33 feet) long, 4 metres (13 feet) high and weigh about 3 tons. However, there is no cause for alarm: although they cannot be brought into the average home, they are gentle creatures, pre-eminently suitable for farming, who will harm no one unless provoked. They are not very bright, having a brain weighing about one twenty-thousandth of their body weight, but their

hearts are in the right place. Indeed, the problem with them is that they can become quite affectionate, and they show their affection by hugging its object with their short, strong forelegs. There are still no reports of any fatalities as a result of this, but several people (unused to country ways) have survived only after mouth-to-mouth resuscitation, and in one case at least this was performed, haphazardly but effectively, by the very hadrosaur who had administered the knock-out squeeze. So, play hard to get, always be ready to run, and don't let your duck-bills get too involved with children or pensioners.

If you own a few hundred acres of woodland (not necessarily pine forest, as you have probably been taught), the feeding can be cheap, although you will need to heat their shed in winter. Hadrosaurs breed readily in captivity, laying their eggs in large communal nests. The meat is good, very much like frog without those irritating little bones. Instead of building a shed specially, you may find it simpler to convert an existing structure, such as a ballroom, church or moat. Keep your hadrosaurs in mixed-sex groups of about half a dozen, where their benevolently episcopal appearance, their gentle nature and their wholesome lack of initiative will be a continual source of delight.

You may, if you choose, farm their eggs: most dinosaur eggs taste very like ostrich eggs and have become a fashionable, if specialized, delicacy, fetching high prices. The present vogue is for serving them hard-boiled with a dinosaur-egg mayonnaise: one egg provides at least four portions. Dinosaur egg boxes will soon be available. Other ways of serving and eating them may be found under *Anatosaurus*.

Many farmers will take the opportunity to diversify: use dinosaurs to clear scrub from fields; docile individuals may be used instead of, or as well as, tractors. Tourism is now an important facet of many farmers' businesses – display your dinosaurs. Dino-rides for children provide a very profitable sideline (don't forget the insurance!); use your imagination! Children love dinosaurs, but may never have seen them in the flesh: make real their dreams.

Saltoposuchus

'Dancing Crocodile', from Latin salto *(dance) + Greek* σουχος *(crocodile), from an advertising gimmick that failed.*

A seductive pseudosuchian whose temptations should be resisted by the fond parent looking for a pet. Leave it to the intensive small meat farmer in search of a challenge.

This thecodont differs from its relative *Euparkeria* in being fully bipedal; it runs, walks and stands on its hind legs, like a kangaroo. Unlike a kangaroo, *Saltoposuchus* does not hop or jump: it runs on its toes, balancing with the help of its tail. Its hind legs are much bigger than the front ones, as you might expect, the front ones being used only to grab food. It is much more active than *Euparkeria*, too. From the nape of its neck to the tip of its long, powerful tail there are rows of little bony plates protecting its back.

Television personalities and other socially mobile characters in search of the next smart pet should remain faithful to the phlegmatic *Stegoceras*. Although it is relatively small, and to that extent fairly manageable, *Saltoposuchus* is an active predator and is not easily tamed. It should go without saying that parents should think twice before deciding to have *Saltoposuchus* as well as children. It is less obvious, but becoming increasingly clear, that *Saltoposuchus*, although not yet regularly bred, is essentially a thecodont that should be kept for meat rather than as a pet. Unhappily, some C-list celebrities have tried to appear in public with a 'tame' *Saltoposuchus*, with predictable results. Although one of these has made the most of the opportunities offered by the experience and gone on to a very successful, if seasonal, career playing Captain Hook in pantomime, others have been less fortunate, having to rely on Social Security or shrewd marriage to keep remaining parts of body and soul together.

Saltoposuchus has quickly become one of the most sought-after dinosaur meats: it is as tender as lamb and divides neatly into joints. Roasting it gives off a mouth-watering aroma that has a succulence reminiscent of gavial. The meat makes the very best dinoburgers and steak tartare. In my view, *Saltoposuchus* is an excellent proposition for any farmer with a smallholding who is in search of a new goal in life. Whereas the big farmer, the type who aims to supply supermarkets,

will be content to raise a straightforward, no-nonsense *Saltoposuchus* for the mass market, the small man will be able to supply a more discerning market by rearing his animals to cater for fashionable tastes. The melange of taste experiences that can be produced by feeding your *Saltoposuchus* on lamb, or on calves, or on goose-livers can command the very highest returns on a relatively moderate investment.

Feeding: *Saltoposuchus* is just as carnivorous as *Euparkeria* and likes plenty of good, meaty food, preferably in large chunks. It is quite uninterested in vegetable matter. Try fish.

Housing: Because it is small, it can be intensively farmed, rather like mink or fox, and the same sort of diet will do. (Please be aware that animal welfare regulations make *Saltoposuchus* farms more economical in countries such as Iraq or Albania than in more socially advanced areas.)

Breeding: Irregular: try methods used for Gila Monster or Mexican Beaded Lizard.

Availability: *Saltoposuchus* at the moment is terribly difficult to find.

Plateosaurus

'Flat Lizard', from Greek πλατύς *(flat)* + σαυρος *(lizard), from an early
belief that these dinosaurs were suitable to be kept in apartment blocks.*

Ideal for the part-time or career farmer who is looking for an opportunity to
diversify. Great satisfaction is to be gained from getting them to mate successfully.

Plateosaurus is a large dinosaur that normally walks
on all fours but will stand on its hind legs to reach
high vegetation, or when running. It is a social
animal, living in herds. On the thumb and first two
fingers are claws: in the male the thumb claw is very
much enlarged and is used in various kinds of sexual
encounter (see below).
Feeding: *Plateosaurus* has flat teeth and lives on
soft vegetation. If you have a small lake, *Plateosaurus*
can be kept in an adjacent field and will crop the
water plants.
Housing: *Plateosaurus* can be kept either near a
lake, or in parkland with shrubs. Fence the lake:
these creatures can swim! Although hedges are
ineffective as fencing, electric fences about 2
metres (6 ½ feet) high usually work well enough.
Breeding: For breeding, males need to be
introduced, and some problems may arise. They are
often rather unmanageable
and the huge thumb-
claw is used as a very
effective weapon. Dosages of
cider have been found to be usefully
incapacitating and beer has a similar effect.
When drunk (20 litres/5 gallons are usually
enough) the male is amiable enough and can be
led by ropes or cables attached to a neck collar.
(His unsteadiness and tendency to fall over can
cause injury to staff, so it is sensible to insure
against this.)

The main obstacle to breeding in these
circumstances is that the male usually finds
successful copulation very difficult. Serious
breeders should construct a breeding pen,
stoutly built, to which the cider-mellowed male
may be led and confined; when he is sober, females
can be led to him at intervals throughout the day
or, if the flock is large, throughout the week. If you
construct a series of compartments, one female can
be manoeuvred out while the male's attention is

distracted by a new female from another direction.
The best aphrodisiac is variety.

The act of mating in *Plateosaurus* is a hit-and-miss
affair: co-operation from the female is essential.
The male must court the female. The function of
courtship here is to bring the female into a mood of
eager participation. The male's display is impressive:
rearing on his hind legs and swaying from side to
side, he inflates a pair of sacs on either side of his
throat. The skin of these becomes congested with
blood and the throat enlarges and becomes red.
At the same time, he bellows continuously, the sacs
acting as resonators. This display eventually results
in the female becoming excited and indicating her
willingness to mate. The male uses his thumb-claw
to get a good grip on his partner: fertile females
have scars on their shoulders; virgins have none.
Availability: Easy to get hold of. Apart from
the traditional auction houses of Trössingen and
Halberstadt in Germany and La Chassagne in France,
perfectly acceptable animals can be obtained in
England and Switzerland.

Psittacosaurus

'PARROT LIZARD', from Greek ψιττακος (parrot) + σαυρος (lizard), from its tendency
to imitate its companions' calls.

Here is a perfectly decent dinosaur for the family, and brimful
of eggs. It can bite, so don't play silly games with it.

A parrot-faced dinosaur up to a couple of metres
(6 ½ feet) long, *Psittacosaurus* has big hands for
grasping plants, a big beak for cropping them and
big teeth for chewing them. Little Red Riding
Hood would have been able to have nice chats with
Psittacosaurus, but the rest of us find it a little boring.
It is both quadrupedal and bipedal. Cocks are needed
to fertilize the hens, otherwise no eggs are produced.
When not employed in this useful task, they may be
hired out to environmental groups for scrub clearance.
Feeding: It eats tough plants, such as shrubs and
small trees, which it chops up with its beak. If you
don't have these plants growing in the dinosaur's
enclosure, you should provide them fresh.

Housing: Keep your *Psittacosaurus* in groups of, say,
half a dozen in a small field and fence it well.
Breeding: If you want them to lay eggs or breed
(probably the only reason to keep them), provide the
same conditions as for *Protoceratops* (p. 57). Remove
eggs the same day they are laid in the nest, which the
dinosaur builds itself: it will then lay more for you.
Even so, the number it will lay is limited: deep-freeze
the eggs after hard-boiling, to ensure a regular supply.
Availability: *Psittacosaurus*, like *Protoceratops*, can
be obtained from the Oshih Formation Company in
Mongolia; those with contact with the Russian mafia
will be able to get hold of specimens more cheaply.

Hypsilophodon

'HIGH RIDGE TOOTH', from Greek υψηλος (high), + λοφος (ridge) + οδους (tooth): the
teeth can be ground up with yeast, sugar and water to produce a fermented drink, marketed
in Australia, called High Ridge Tooth.

A very manageable source of winter eggs. Tame, friendly and
adaptable – but don't expect it to climb trees!

This little charmer is usually less than 2 metres
(6 ½ feet) long and easily obtained from the Isle
of Wight. It has rows of bony plates in the skin of
its back and is bipedal, with a long, stiff tail that it
uses to balance itself, particularly when running,
which it does very quickly and very often. If you
obtain one as a chick, your *Hypsilophodon* becomes
tame and friendly, although it is naturally timid and
prone to panic. It is suitable for children and will
enjoy winning races with them but, like so many
early Cretaceous ornithopods, it is impossible to
house-train.
Feeding: It has a row of small teeth on its upper jaw
at the front of its mouth and eats fruit and leaves. It

will not eat grass: make fresh food available
to it at all times, soft rather than hard.
Housing: *Hypsilophodon* needs space: it is a highly
agile and speedy sprinter and if confined it becomes
constipated, mopes and dies. Do not make the
common mistake of crowding its enclosure with
trees: it doesn't climb trees; it cannot climb trees.
Breeding: Keep it outdoors in summer and in a big,
heated enclosure in winter: eggs are sure to come.
Availability: *Hypsilophodon* is one of Britain's most
easily obtained dinosaurs. The best specimens are to
be found in department stores on the Isle of Wight,
where prices are lowest. Otherwise, you could try
the classified ads.

Protoceratops

'EARLIEST HORNY EYE', from Greek πρῶτος (earliest) + κέρας (horn) + ὄψις (vision), from its habit of mating at dawn.

An easily fed dinosaur that lays large numbers of eggs; conveniently paddocked in scrub in summer and housed indoors in winter. Quite easily bred.

At just over 2 metres (6 ½ feet) long, *Protoceratops* is a relatively small dinosaur and (together with *Leptoceratops*, p. 25) by far the easiest of the frilled ones. It has no horns, only a small frill, and is a quadruped.

If you want to use the eggs as food, make sure that you gather them soon after laying and eat them soon after gathering. They don't like having their eggs taken away and in the wild commonly fight with those who try to raid their nests. They may get used to losing them in time, but at first it is advisable to take the eggs under cover of darkness, although you may risk treading on a slumbering parent; better still, create a diversion. This should not be anything that will make them panic, as fireworks surely will; rather some spectacle without too great a surprise element, such as a video of *Jurassic Park*. They will stand still and gape, leaving you quite safe to take their eggs.

One last word: the jaws of *Protoceratops* are extremely strong, and the beak extremely sharp. Be sober, be vigilant, or you will lose a finger, or even a hand.

Feeding: *Protoceratops* is totally herbivorous and easily fed: it likes tough stuff, such as entire shrubs. In temperate climates you can enclose them in a hectare (couple of acres) or so of scrubland, where they will be happy tucking into bramble, hawthorn, blackthorn and so on.

Housing: Bring them indoors in winter. The floor should be well-drained: if it is concrete, it must have a good, thick covering of sand, sawdust or peat.

Breeding: For maximum egg-production, strip lighting is best and fluorescent cheapest to run. Provide heat spots for sunbathing by installing a spotlight every metre or so.

As long as both sexes are present they will, a few days after their early-morning mating, lay large numbers of large eggs in large nests, which they scrape in the ground. *Protoceratops* relies on the heat of the sun to incubate the eggs. If you live in a cool area, you must carefully unearth the eggs and incubate them artificially. Most airing cupboards are far too small. You will need a large, warm, moist chamber for successful breeding: a sauna is ideal.

The eggshells are leathery: you can detect undesirable hard-shelled eggs by their unexpected heaviness, together with an unexpected opacity. This hard shell causes late hatching as well as problems for anyone wanting to eat them. Moisten the eggs daily (twice daily when humidity is low) with warm water.

Rearing the chicks is best left to the parents if at all possible. Watch carefully: if either parent shows hostility, you may have to do the rearing yourself. Expect problems and use common sense.

Availability: *Protoceratops* can be obtained from the Djadochta Markets in the Gobi Desert; unfortunately, because of the lax animal husbandry regulations there, many specimens are damaged through close encounter with *Velociraptors*, which all too often break into their holding cages.

Iguanodon

'IGUANA TOOTH', from Arawak iwana *(iguana) via Spanish* iguana *(iguana) + Greek* ὀδούς *(tooth). Iguana Tooth was the familiar name given to this animal by the expatriate farmers of the Greater Antilles and British Guiana (now Guyana).*

Docile to the point of soppiness, compliant, herdable and full of meat. Ideal for the farmer with parkland. Unsuitable as a pet.

Iguanodon is a big dinosaur, 10 metres (33 feet) long and 5 metres (16 feet) high, and it is mainly bipedal. It has a long tongue and a horny beak; on each hand there are four fingers, with hooves, and a thumb with a powerful spine. On each foot there are three toes, with sharp hooves. Ex-cattle farmers wanting to change their focus should not be dismayed by the size of *Iguanodon*, for the creature is not only docile but also amiable. Indeed, because of its size and tractability and the tastiness of its meat – somewhere between pork and lobster – *Iguanodon* is an ideal dinosaur for meat farming.

Feeding: The animals herd naturally and will eat almost all greenery (with the exception of grass), using their many rows of leaf-shaped teeth.

Housing: Like cattle, they should be enclosed to prevent their straying onto public roads, where they may cause major traffic delays. Like cows and sheep, you can lead them along the public highway, as long as you keep them orderly and to one side of the road. Remember that they are easily startled and may be panicked by fast-moving cars or impatient motorists sounding their horns. For this reason, it is best to move them late at night. A startled *Iguanodon* likes to use its thumb-spike as a weapon and so it must be awakened very gently: don't ring bells in their ears, throw buckets of cold water over their heads or shine bright lights in their eyes. Treat them as you would a child: shake them gently by the shoulder and quietly murmur something like, 'Time to get up, old girl: we're going on a journey'. You may have to shake and murmur for several minutes.

It is quite impossible to wake a flock single-handed: by the time the second one is awake the first will have squatted down and gone back to sleep. You need a waker for each *Iguanodon*: either hire freelance nightworkers (asylum-seekers are ideal) or, a popular ploy among the wealthier gentleman-farmers, throw a Dinosaur Wake. Give your guests just one drink on arrival and, when they are all assembled, explain the procedure – stressing the importance of a gentle touch. Then lead them out to your pasture and ask each guest to wake an *Iguanodon*. When all are fully awake, the *Iguanodon* are lead to their new pasture and the assembled company returns to the farmhouse where you serve more drinks and charcoal-grilled *Iguanodon* steaks.

A prize – often a haunch of *Iguanodon* for the (industrial-size) freezer – is awarded to the guest with the most original line in dinosaur pillow talk. Such parties are becoming very popular. The Dinosaur Hoof, a rather clumsy dance in which the participants wear Wellington boots and evening dress, originated at dinosaur wakes in Texas.

Breeding: Regular and often.

Availability: After a period in which the Bernissart Iguanodon Emporium in Belgium seemed the only outlet for *Iguanodon*, the market has become more liberal, thanks to the European Commission, and herds are now also available in Germany (Nehden) and England (Sussex and Kent).

Camptosaurus

'BENT LIZARD', from Greek κάμπτω *(bend, bow, turn around, make someone alter his or her sentiments)* + σαυρος *(lizard), from its social malleability.*

A straightforward and trouble-free dinosaur for the farmer with plenty of scrub. Fairly manageable but not really suitable for the apartment-dweller.

Camptosaurus, which is pleasantly mottled, walks on two or four legs, according to its mood. It is surprising that so few farmers have turned to it (its Greek name κάμπτω means 'Make Someone Alter His or Her Sentiments'). The conditions needed for commercial exploitation of *Plateosaurus* (see p. 55) should also be suitable for *Camptosaurus*. In fact, the male of *Camptosaurus* is far more manageable than that of *Plateosaurus*, particularly if kept sober, and may be treated like a female (κάμπτω!). The meat is excellent, reminiscent of crocodile and more tender than *Plateosaurus*, and, because it is still relatively scarce, it fetches good prices from the recently established chains of dinosaur butchers.

Feeding and Housing: Basically, it is a browser, so you can't just put a flock in a field and forget about it. It has a horny beak at the front of the mouth, rather like a cow's, ridged, closely-packed teeth for chopping and crushing tough vegetation, like a cow's, and cheeks which store cropped food and push food between the teeth for grinding, like a cow's. But, unlike a cow, it cannot digest grass. *Camptosaurus* prefers the leaves of low-growing plants, so the would-be *Camptosaurus*-farmer is hard put to find an economic food. Chamomile lawns have been suggested, but according to many farmers, this is not realistic. Grassland turning to scrub is a good bet: *Camptosaurus* will greedily take nettles, thistles, brambles, elder, hawthorn and so on (particularly young plants) and so is useful at clearing weed-infested former pastureland. You will probably need to move your flock from pasture to pasture fairly frequently. A Dinosaur Wake (see opposite) is the best way, although Camptosaurus Wakes have less social clout than Iguanodon Wakes. *Camptosaurus*

are usually well-behaved, particularly at night in public places.

Like so many things 7 metres (23 feet) long, *Camptosaurus* is really for the farmer rather than the apartment-dweller.

Breeding: Breeding is straightforward and trouble-free. Mating occurs in the summer, out in the open. Courtship in cool climates is subtle and inconspicuous but nevertheless necessary (κάμπτω again). In warmer climates courtship becomes more florid, and the same is true in the case of *Camptosaurus*. The sexes are not easily distinguished: there is no difference that can be easily seen. Use your intuition, therefore: males have a maleness that is indefinable but undeniable. Eggs are laid about a year after fertilization.

Availability: After some years, when the only way to get specimens was through the overpriced dinosaur-auctions of South Dakota and Utah, it is now possible to get them from the Oxford-based Cumnor Dinomart and, via the Internet, from a Portuguese site.

700kg
1,545lb

Riojasaurus

'Rioja Lizard' from Rioja + Greek σαυρος (lizard), after its liking for Spanish wine.

Think of this useful prosauropod as the South American equivalent of *Plateosaurus* (p. 55). It can be profitably farmed there, either like *Plateosaurus* or free-range on the pampas.

Right: Riojasaurus burgers, coming soon to a supermarket near you.

To picture this dinosaur, think of *Plateosaurus* with a beak. The meat is easily canned and corned, and it is likely that *Riojasaurus* will be the third of the three styles of dinoburger – *Iguanodon* and *Camptosaurus* have already been chosen – soon to be launched in a blaze of publicity (a hundred *Gallimimus* and a chorus line of *Longisquama* are already in training) by a leading burger chain.

Riojasaurus can be trained, by the sound of a horn, to return from its pampas to its shelter in the evening. It might well be trained to respond to a range of tunes with a range of different activities, allowing a dinosaur farmer with a sophisticated sound system to live the indolent life of a disc jockey.

Feeding: In South America they browse free-range on the local pampas-grass. It is astonishing how *Riojasaurus* manages to survive on a diet as tough as pampas-grass. Perhaps its penchant for red wine and the symbiotic bacteria that live in the gut help in the tricky business of digesting this tough reed.

Housing: Like *Plateosaurus*, *Riojasaurus* thrives best outdoors, but you need to provide suitable shelters to which the flock can retire at night or in bad weather.

Breeding: See 'Hadrosaurs' (p. 53).

Availability: *Riojasaurus* is available only in South America at present, with the best and cheapest specimens obtained from corner shops in Northwest Argentina.

Anatosaurus

'Duck Lizard', from Greek νήσσα (duck), via Latin anas + Greek σαυρος (lizard), from its habit of submerging its fellow dinosaurs in the water.

Arguably the best hadrosaurs for the farmer familiar with sandy soil; big, gentle and easily bred, they can also be decorative in safari parks and are wonderful layers.

Anatosaurus is a delightful hadrosaur. With no crest, it is a typical flat-headed duck-bill, which likes to swim. Give it water in large quantities: remember, it likes to immerse its friends under water, so take precautions.

Anatosaurus eggs are about 23 centimetres (9 inches) long and notoriously hard to get into. The leathery shell gets very tough when it is cooked: use an electric drill and help the contents out with a small fork. Few English or American restaurants are prepared to offer entire *Anatosaurus* eggs, but in France many bistros now serve soft-boiled eggs (be prepared for a half-hour wait) with a baguette to dip in. They provide rotary, diamond-tipped cutters: to

enter, engrave a circle, strike the cut area with a hammer and lift away with a rubber suction pad. A patent dinosaur egg-opener is available in top-end department stores and works like a wall-mounted can-opener. A table version, incorporating a dinosaur egg cup and reservoirs for salt and pepper, has already been tested on a random sample of the public.

Feeding: It is a catholic browser and will eat seeds, fruit and twigs.

Housing and Breeding: See 'Hadrosaurs' (p. 53).

Availability: *Anatosaurus*, like most hadrosaurs, is relatively easy to find in North America, although Canada remains the retail centre.

Parasaurolophus

'Beside Lizard Ridge', from Greek παρά (beside) + σαυρος (lizard) + λόφος (ridge), from the crest of rock where the best specimens are found.

Ideal for farmers living on otherwise uninhabited islands. Easily fed and cared for, a wonderful source of eggs, meat and company for the hard of hearing.

This majestic dinosaur bears a crest more than 2 metres (6 ½ feet) long. With an overall length of 10 metres (33 feet) and immense fertility, it is the most valuable hadrosaur for both meat and eggs. However, it has one major drawback: it is very noisy. The hollow crest contains the air passage from lungs to mouth and acts as an acoustic resonator. The booming bellows of this extrovert dinosaur make farming it possible only in remote areas, far from human habitation.

Like so many of the dinosaurs, *Parasaurolophus* has a sense of humour and a love of surprise. If, like so many farmers, you are of a gentle, contemplative nature and like from time to time to stand quietly musing on a flower or to sit in some private nook reading a favourite poem, *Parasaurolophus* may not be for you. He will seek you out, creep stealthily behind you, put his mouth to your ear, hold his breath for an instant then let out a primaeval honk, similar to the foghorn of a supertanker.

Despite this, a cult of *Parasaurolophus* fanciers is flourishing, and the Friends of Parasaurolophus Society (FOPS) now has branches in several countries. FOPS tell me that, in spite of several postponements, they will be launching a programme of *Parasaurolophus* shows regularly in remote places. Enthusiasts and their dinosaurs will travel the long distances involved in specially soundproofed pantechnicons. Males will be judged on the volume of their calls as well as the size and shape of their crests; females will be judged, as usual, on the regularity of their features and the colouring of their skin markings. Account will be taken in both sexes of the clarity of the eyes, which are some 10 centimetres (4 inches) across, and eggs will be judged for size and colouring. These events will obviously be very colourful and an excellent day out for people with limited conversational skills; all

participants will be issued with ear plugs and need to communicate in sign language.

Feeding: See 'Hadrosaurs' (p. 53).
Housing: See 'Hadrosaurs' (p. 53).
Breeding: See 'Hadrosaurs' (p. 53).
Availability: *Parasaurolophus* are not difficult to obtain in Canada and the U.S.A.; connoisseurs will want to visit the Hadrostore in Albuquerque, New Mexico, where the trade flourishes and exchanges can be arranged.

Kentrosaurus

'PAIN LIZARD', from Greek κεντρον *(instrument of torture)*
+ σαυρος *(lizard), from the sensation caused by the tail.*

Here is a stegosaur that is ideal
for a farmer with a few hundred
hectares of tropical swamp.
Almost self-maintaining,
Kentrosaurus is easily bred
and aimable enough.

Although you will by now be used to Internet sites,
particularly American ones, advertising *Kentrosaurus*
at 'a magnificent 15-foot-long', you will be lucky to
obtain one any longer than 3 metres (10 feet); it is
one of the smallest stegosaurs. It is still a prickly
customer, however, with pairs of long spikes attached
to the skin of its back and tail, one pair of which juts
out sideways at its hips. The first six or so pairs are
flattened and have a good blood supply, just as in
Stegosaurus (p. 79). The others are for defence,
particularly the ones on the tail: these are used as
weapons when *Kentrosaurus* wants to drive off
real or (more often) imagined enemies. It is amiable
but obtuse. If things seem unexpected (and nearly
everything that happens is totally unexpected to
Kentrosaurus), it lashes out with its spiked tail.

The other problem is housing. This stegosaur
catches cold easily and in temperate climates you
cannot allow it to stand outside if there is an R
in the month, even if the sun is shining. Also,
Kentrosaurus is prone to Stegosaur Pox (see p. 93)

Although *Kentrosaurus* is civil enough and friendly
to those it learns to recognize as its friends, or even
acquaintances, its brain continually lets it down.
Memories fade rapidly and yesterday's friend is today's
menacing stranger. I referred earlier to the nervous
swipes of its spiky tail: not even a suit of armour will
protect you. In your relations with stegosaurs the
golden rule is: stop short of intimacy. This rule may
be bent by hardy farmers in the case of *Scelidosaurus*
(p.78), but with *Kentrosaurus* (and, of course, with
Stegosaurus itself) you have to show restraint.
Feeding: As in all stegosaurs, feeding can be a
problem. Moss-like plants such as horsetails and
similar soft foods are all that *Kentrosaurus* can chew.

Housing and Breeding: Do not take on the
husbandry of *Kentrosaurus* unless you have at least
10 hectares (25 acres) of horsetail-infested swamp;
surround it with a good mud wall at least 2 metres
(6 ½ feet) high and with an electrically heated,
thermostatically controlled enclosure.

You might think that few dinosaurs are less
suitable for meat farming than *Kentrosaurus*. But
one man's mite is another man's foison: what we
in the developed world find most difficult about
Kentrosaurus are feeding it and keeping it warm.
No such problems are found in the swamps of
Central Africa. The Sudd in Sudan, for example, is
ideal for stegosaurs: it is one of the world's largest
tropical freshwater swamps and parts of it could
easily be enclosed and adapted for a flock. The
climate is ideal for them, food abounds and your
Kentrosaurus will flourish. A further advantage is
this: stegosaurs will not usually breed in captivity,
but this dim dinosaur does not associate a swamp
with captivity, chicks are produced regularly and
numbers increase. Once a good-sized flock has built
up, individuals can be culled as required. Such a
farm almost runs itself and will be a boon to the
protein-starved Third World. Much of the above
applies with equal force to *Scelidosaurus* and
Stegosaurus, but the future of stegosaur farming
in tropical freshwater swamps bounded by mud
walls and with labourers' huts on stilts still lies
first and foremost with *Kentrosaurus*.
Availability: Tendaguru Hill Farm Supplies in
Tanzania still offers the best bargain *Kentrosaurus*,
though many are disappointingly small.

450kg
992lb

7 | DINOSAURS FOR HIDE AND FEATHER

Romantics will want to keep dinosaurs for their own sake, but there will always be those who will want to make money out of them. And why not? Dinosaur hides, pelts and plumage are as fashionable as they ever have been, and I have suggested *Longisquama* as a good starting point for the feather enthusiast, even though he may later graduate to the more expensive *Incisivosaurus*. However, the clever money is in hides.

For all heavy leather products the ankylosaurs are unbeatable. For those who are keen on tanks, nothing presses the button like an ankylosaur: heavy, well-armoured, slow, expensive to run and occasionally deadly. Quite what the attraction of these almost reptilian creatures is remains a mystery to me, but they do show that there is a dinosaur to suit (almost) every taste. By dinosaur standards they are not all that difficult to keep. The golden rule is: *keep away from the tail*, especially if you have *Ankylosaurus.*

Feeding arrangements are the same for all of them. As a general rule the slower and more heavily armoured they are, the less fussy they are with their food. Horsetails of the vegetable kind are a good basic, but you should supplement these with soft vegetables and soft fruit. Try commercial cake, deciduous leaves, soft bark, cabbage, peaches, pomegranates, pineapples or passion-fruit.

Breeding success is spasmodic: it makes good

economic sense to encourage it, so try whatever seems likely to turn them on. Many farmers have found it worthwhile to install a sprinkler system – many dinosaurs are brought into the mood by rain; others find that it is cheaper and more effective to install a cheap but powerful sound system – mood music to set the hormones racing. Try boogy-woogy or Stravinsky's 'Infernal Dance of King Kashchei'.

If eggs are laid, what should you do with them? You cannot ignore the problems that are likely to occur when you try to take away the fruits of maternity from a fractious female; equally, you must look at the best commercial outcome for your business. If you want to expand your flock, let the mother hatch her eggs. If you want a little upmarket sideline, collect the eggs and sell them, either to visitors in your own farm shop or café, or to a third party (Eggs R Us and East Coast Easy Ova are both up and running). The techniques you can use to get hold of the eggs are many and ingenious; however, I suggest you use that splendid old tried and tested stand-by, the anaesthetic dart. Make sure you don't shoot the female when she is standing above the eggs.

For the summer months your ankylosaurs will do best outside. Excavate a pit to the depth of about a metre (3 feet), then enclose it with a brick wall high enough to keep the animals in; 3 metres (10 feet) should do. Then drive steel sheets in to a depth of a metre (3 feet), right around the perimeter, to prevent escape by burrowing. Line the enclosure with at least one metre (3 feet) of concrete: the club-tailed ankylosaurs can demolish most walls in a few seconds. Inside the enclosure supply plenty of loose, friable soil and some largish boulders to provide adequate hiding places for nervous individuals: remember, a twitchy ankylosaur is a destructive ankylosaur. There must be an abundant supply of water for drinking and cooling. A heated indoor pit of similar design should be provided for winter.

Ankylosaur hide is extremely tough and difficult to bend, but it is proof against some bullets, so the trend amongst film and pop stars for covering cars with it is not just a publicity-seeking affectation. The spikes, plates, warts and nodules, which the superstars leave on, can be filed off to produce durable saddles for *Ornithomimus* or horses and excellent knee pads for those who clean floors in the traditional way. Many crash-helmets are now made from ankylosaur hides and there is a great deal of interest in using them as non-slip covering for surfboards, flight-decks of aircraft carriers and other similar objects. Hide is definitely the direction the sensible farmer will go with ankylosaurs. After some disappointing trials in Ho Chi Minh City, the verdict of the jury of specialized chefs was this: do not bother with the meat. No amount of cooking can make it remotably chewable. Zoos can, of course, feed it raw to carnosaurs like *Tyrannosaurus* and also the less fussy raptors and pterosaurs.

The six most popular ankylosaur species are discussed below. All but *Ankylosaurus*, which is

too difficult to manage, are shown in competitions, where they are judged on the quality of their armour. Ankylosaur shows used to be held in disused reservoirs, which could be easily modified to make escape-proof show rings. Now that owners have more confidence in their ankylosaur obedience-training techniques, most shows are taking place in towns and cities, where the local football or athletics stadium, once the temporary barriers have been installed, have proved perfectly adequate in terms of safety, and far more convenient for the spectators. We have even had the unwelcome appearance of a streaker at one of these shows, unwelcome because it sparked off a panic among the *Tarchia*, who demolished the Members' Stand.

Do not go away with the idea that only the ankylosaurs can be farmed for their skins. Other dinosaurs have their parts to play. The general usefulness of *Therizinosaurus* is secondary to its beautiful feathery coat. Pterosaur skins are very fashionable at present: casual wear featuring the combination of the furry body-skin and the fur-free wing membranes is now proving a great hit with the more vigorous young holiday-makers in the clubs and on the beaches of the Balearics, especially after the publication of a Papal Bull banning its use in the Vatican. Many a police dino-handler has been able to sell the skin of his *Coelophysis* or *Ornitholestes*, once it has reached retirement age, to supplement his police pension: the skins are used to make such items as ladies' jackets, heavy-duty umbrellas and novelty telephone-covers.

Therizinosaurus

'Decapitator Lizard', from Greek θεριζω *(cut off)* + ινιον *(neck, nape)* + σαυρος *(lizard); this name has arisen from a few overpublicized cases when irresponsible farm workers have been beheaded.*

A multi-purpose agricultural dinosaur popular for its many virtues in and around the farm, although safety measures are advised.

Only lately have the virtues of this multi-talented beast been recognized. In China, that most populous of countries, its powdered claws have been valued as an aphrodisiac for millennia. In England, the farmers and squires of the shires, confident in their own fertility, have concentrated on more profitable uses and have clasped *Therizinosaurus* to their collective agricultural bosom with all the zeal of a convert. And well they might: just look at the animal and what it can do!

At 12 metres (39 feet) long, and walking on its hind legs, *Therizinosaurus* is about the size of *Tyrannosaurus*, with enormous, scythe-shaped, bony claws on its arms; however, far from being a mean meat-eating machine, *Therizinosaurus* is a gentle herbivore, using its claws to rake in leaves and branches from trees and bushes. It likes nothing better than to amble around, grabbing armfuls of leafy vegetation, which it then stuffs into its toothless beak. So why keep it?

Why not? Its beautiful feathery coat, with its often startling patterns, is in great demand in the boutiques of the Pacific Rim, and will almost certainly take the European fashion houses by storm: scarves, cloaks, skirts, trousers, hats, coats… In fact, all items of clothing (except, perhaps, underwear, where the more robust plumes still cause problems) are eagerly awaited by the chic and famous.

Even before it is slaughtered and skinned for the benefit of the young and trendy, *Therizinosaurus* is the farmer's friend: although females are not bountiful egg-providers, the farmer's wife is usually adept at taking advantage of an occasional clutch. It can be harnessed to implements and used as a tractor; it can be used to clear shrubs or to pull down trees. Its arms and claws are already useful in open-cast mining and, if properly trained, *Therizinosaurus* can be used in the construction industry for deconstruction, replacing the less adaptable bulldozer and JCB. Well-insured farmers with efficient training regimes for both dinosaurs and human workers find *Therizinosaurus* a

very profitable investment: if it is trained from infancy, its sickle-like claws can be used to shear sheep or to reap crops of all kinds at harvest time (although this is where most accidents occur, as poorly trained farm-workers get too close to the swinging scythes of the enthusiastic dinosaurs and lose their heads). And when the grim reaper itself harvests these inoffensive giants, the farmer can sell the meat to the big dinoburger chains.

Feeding: *Therizinosaurus* is so big that feeding costs are considerable unless the owner has a riverside wood that needs reclamation, or a large, scrubby hillside. Concentrates, including urea $(CO(NH_2)_2)$, are being used in some farms, but often result in excessive methane (CH_4) production (see Constipation, p. 92).

Housing: This is unexpectedly easy for a large dinosaur: because *Therizinosaurus* is (relatively) warm-blooded and has a feathery coat, the heating costs are minimal. Shelter from rain and wind is required, but aircraft hangars make excellent barns. Thought should be given to disposal of manure.

Breeding: This is very haphazard: a female will lay an occasional clutch of eggs, which she may or may not decide to incubate. If she does, you have an opportunity to train the babies from a very early age and implant skills that will enable you to exploit the power and scything skills of this dinosaur: road-building, house-demolition, canal-construction and estate-management leap to mind.

Availability: The Nemegt Basin, Bath and Toilet Centre in southern Inner Mongolia breeds *Therizinosaurus* as a profitable sideline; otherwise, try the Asian Feather-Farmers Co-operatives in Khazakhstan or Transbaykalia.

Left: Therizinosaurus, *a herbivore in wolf's clothing, makes an enthusiastic sheep shearer when suitably trained from an early age.*

Longisquama

'LONG SCALE', from Latin longus *(long)* + squama *(scale),*
from its musical talents.

A friendly little fellow, brightly coloured and covered with feathery frills. Not
difficult to feed and thrives in company. For feathery frills and feathery thrills.

The 'feathers' are used mainly for sexual display, by
both *Longisquama* and the world of fashion. The
animal itself is a tiny thecodont – much smaller than
the spurious 1-metre- (3-foot-) long specimens
advertised twenty years ago – with a curious
appearance: it is covered with scales, some of which
have the appearance of feathers, projecting like little
frills. But the most striking feature of *Longisquama* is
the row of long scales above its backbone from neck
to pelvis. These are brightly coloured and can be
raised or lowered.

Longisquama is yet another charmer: it is friendly
and generally unaggressive, enjoying playing with
children and being taken for walks. However, it
is not very intelligent and the only trick it can be
taught – by rewarding it with dragonflies or tinned
peaches – is to raise its scaly crest on command. If
you can train a troupe of, say, six *Longisquama* to
raise and lower their crests in unison and to music,
you will find yourself greatly in demand on the home
entertainment circuit. Start them off on the slowest
music you can find: any Leonard Cohen number or
Otto Klemperer recording will do. Move on to
waltzes and ballads ('The Blue Danube' or 'Grandad'
spring to mind) and when the muscles really develop
try 'The Flight of the Bumble Bee' or 'Rock Around
the Clock'.

Although *Longisquama* has only one trick in its
repertoire you can exploit it in various ways. For
example, at fashionable gatherings such as Ascot or a
Buckingham Palace Garden Party you can use your
pet, draped fashionably over a shoulder, to signal
coded greetings to your secret lover, who can reply
in kind. At the other end of the social scale, the
imaginative burglar can use his *Longisquama* to act
as a look-out to provide a silent scaly signal when it
spots the police.

It is happiest kept with others in groups of up to
ten. Moulting occurs annually at the end of summer
and this is when you should gather the scaly 'feathers'.

They are strikingly unusual when worn in hats and
to cover the controversial areas of personalities
attending fashionable parties. The longer feathers are
much prized by woodwind players for cleaning their
instruments and annoying the violas.

Longisquama is unfortunately prone to depluming
scabies (see p. 92).

Feeding: It eats fruit, dragonflies and bumble bees: a
bizarre diet. It will accept various commercial brands
of monkey food, as well as eggs and some kitchen
scraps. However, feeding is not as difficult as it seems.

Housing: Give it plenty of shrubs or branches in
its securely roofed pen, and lots of sunshine. In
winter, supplement this with ultraviolet lamps, and
make sure the enclosure is heated: *Longisquama*
is only little.

Breeding: Breeding is simple: pairing
takes place after a spectacular crest-waving
courtship, and seven to nine eggs are
laid in the sand. These should be
artificially heated by UV lamps
if they are to hatch in temperate
countries.

Availability: The best specimens
come from Turkestan, a difficult
place to import dinosaurs from at the
best of times, and some local knowledge
is needed: as so often, the local chiefs
need to be comforted with flagons.

100g
0.2lb

Ankylosaurus

'CROOKED LIZARD', from Greek ἀγκυλος (crooked,) + σαυρος (lizard), from its flawed character.

This disagreeable animal can be kept like any other ankylosaur and might just appeal to a wholesale fruiterer. It is, however, very untrustworthy and a dinosaur to avoid.

Many dinosaur-lovers will be surprised to find the dreaded *Ankylosaurus* included in this book. They rightly regard it as beyond the pale and its adherents as a lunatic fringe who give dinosaur-keeping a bad name. I include it for three reasons: first, it epitomizes its family; second, I feel a duty to warn the unsuspecting; third, like anything thoroughly tasteless, *Ankylosaurus* has enjoyed a brief period of enormous popularity and, in spite of the problems it has caused (the Leaning Tower of Pisa and the partial destruction of the Coliseum in Rome spring to mind), its time, unfortunately, is now.

Superficially, the creature is a squat tank: its back and tail are covered with a carapace of horny plates, and a fringe of large bony spikes projects from its sides, close to and parallel with the ground, surrounding the animal from its neck to the end of its tail, which has a bony knob on its tip. The problems, however, stem from its mental attitude. It is aggressive, foul-tempered, unpredictable, hostile to all other living species, impossible to please, sadistic and uninterested in personal hygiene. Unlike the numerous humans who share these qualities, *Ankylosaurus* has not one redeeming feature. If you must have an *Ankylosaurus* – and do consider *Nodosaurus*, *Polacanthus* or even *Tarchia* first – you must take special precautions at all times and especially when providing food, to avoid death or injury. *Ankylosaurus* has a habit of running sideways (not backwards) at a suspected enemy and impaling him on its spikes. If the intended victim dodges the first lateral onslaught, the spiky tail is brought into play. Legs have been lost this way and plate armour has proved ineffective (see *Dromaeosaurus*, p. 41). Never go within 3 metres (10 foot) of *Ankylosaurus*, always be ready to run (it is slow-moving), and above all make not even the tiniest attempt at friendship: it delights in impaling the soft-hearted.

Ankylosaurus, like other dinosaurs, may suffer from Locomotor Ataxia (see p. 93): ataxia in the largest dinosaurs is the disease most likely to lead to destruction of property. As it is hereditary and incurable, you have an excuse for euthanasia.

Feeding: The usual ankylosaur feeding remarks pertain here, but *Ankylosaurus* is particularly fond of fruit. All berries are useful when in season but for the rest of the year you will have to rely on supermarket fruits. Apples, pears, grapes and mangosteens will be usual stand-bys. Dried currants and raisins that have been soaked in warm water and then drained of surplus moisture are also good. Chopped dates and figs are useful, but sticky, boiled rice or corn is welcomed more churlishly.

Housing: See pages 64–5.

Breeding: See pages 64–5.

Availability: As usual, in spite of the unsuitability of *Ankylosaurus* for captivity, the Dinomarts of Montana, particularly the Hell Creek KT Interface Emporium and some of the auction rooms of Alberta can circumvent all the regulations and obtain specimens for you without difficulty.

Euoplocephalus

'WELL-TOOLED POINT', from Greek εύ- *(well)* + ὅπλον *(tool)* + κεφαλή *(point, head),*
in reference to its fertility.

If you are really careful with its diet and can provide plenty of exercise, this
formidable dinosaur, even allowing for its tendency to constipation, can be easily
assimilated into the tolerant family circle. Very popular among ankylosaurophiles.

Up to 6 metres (20 feet) long and 2 tons in weight,
with a tortoise-like carapace of bony plates over its
back, this dinosaur has a bony lump on its tail, which
it uses like a shillelagh in defence. It is the most
endearing of the ankylosaurs, a relatively sensitive
creature which displays compassion and mercy: it will
not attack an animal smaller than itself, unless very
sorely provoked. Indeed, it will respond to friendly
gestures, such as specially prepared food or a friendly
pat on the head: it particularly loves you to scratch
its armoured eyelids.

Euoplocephalus loves to be taken on walks: keep
it on a leash and, for safety's sake, strap its tail to
its back with a chain fastened around its middle. It
will allow you to do this once it knows that this is
a prelude to a walk. A well-tamed *Euoplocephalus*
will even allow children to ride on its back. This
is perfectly safe, since the creature lumbers rather
slowly along. Because of this combination of

safety and predictability many primary schools
and nurseries are hiring *Euoplocephalus* for sports
day races: even the least agile toddler may be safely
strapped on to the dinosaur's back. Be sure to keep
the charcoal handy!

Feeding: The usual ankylosaur remarks apply to
its diet (see pp. 64–5), but *Euoplocephalus* does like
its food soft. Overboil if necessary. If its diet is not
to its liking, it suffers from indigestion: it is most
important to remember that wood charcoal is
necessary for all dinosaurs in captivity to absorb
gases in the intestine and ward off flatulence, often
a considerable nuisance to owners of the larger
dinosaur species.

Housing: See pages 64–5.

Breeding: Very easily bred (See pages 64–5).

Availability: Red Deer River Retailers of Alberta;
some buyers have managed to get hold of them in
Sinkiang province in China.

Polacanthus

'SUNDIAL SPINE', from Greek πόλς (sundial) + ἄκανθα (spine), from the use of its shoulder spikes to make the gnomons of ceremonial sundials.

A rather ponderous dinosaur covered with spikes, warts and plates. If given its own spacious, centrally-heated pit, it offers unexpected results to the discerning owner.

With *Polacanthus* we get a taste of the grotesquerie so beloved of the ankylosaur-fancier, but the underlying body is still relatively flexible, although thickset. At 4 metres (13 feet) long, it is more of a heavily armoured car than a tank. On its neck, back and shoulders are several pairs of massive spikes, and over its hind legs is a heavy bony plate; its tail is decorated with a double row of vertical bony slabs.

Of all the ankylosaur hides, *Polacanthus* – dividing as it does into three sections – probably makes the most suitable and eye-catching protection for the limousines of heads of state: spikes at the front, bony plate on the roof and vertical slabs at the rear. Some

pop-stars and footballers use polacanthus-hide for the back seats of their cars. The reason for this is not clear.

Feeding: It cannot stand grapes.
Housing: See pages 64–5.
Breeding: See pages 64–5.
Availability: At present limited to the Isle of Wight, and even here you may be offered specimens with bits missing: be careful. Try also the Museum Shop in South Kensington.

Tarchia

'BRAINY', from Greek ταρφύς (thick), an ironic comment on its intelligence.

In *Tarchia* we have a dinosaur for the specialist. It is sullen, cantankerous and prone to constipation. Popular among ankylosaurophiles.

Tarchia consists of 4 tons of bad-tempered, usually motionless armour. It has bony nodules on its back and in appearance it is squat. For a tail it has a club, which it is likely to use at the least provocation, or none. Unlike *Ankylosaurus*, however, it can be lulled into a sleepy form of good humour. It will be transfixed by a metronome, a pendulum, a tennis match or any form of kinetic sculpture. In this state it can be groomed for competition, driven about in heavy-duty transporters and even prodded by judges without retaliating.

The best way to rouse it from its trance is to show it a really striking piece of op art: the more affluent farmers always keep one or two Bridget

Riley paintings in the back of the van just for this purpose.

Wear armour if you have to go close to it, although even this will not protect you against anything more than a lazy or playful glancing blow.
Feeding: If you deviate from the menu I suggest (see p. 64), constipation may result (see p. 92). You can usually cure it by giving extra greens and fruits.
Housing: See pages 64–5.
Breeding: See pages 64–5.
Availability: Mongolian horse markets, particularly near Barun Goyot in the south.

Nodosaurus

'GIRDLE LIZARD', from Latin nodus *(girdle)* + *Greek* σαυρος *(lizard),*
from the use of its bony plates to make corsets.

The fussiest but least dangerous ankylosaur. Although children should be kept away, it will quickly get to know its owner and has an unexpectedly charming nature.

Nodosaurus is the most manageable ankylosaur. Its armour consists of bony plates and warts rather than spikes (as in *Polacanthus*, p. 71). Once it is familiar with someone, it will allow them to clean its cage, and even the floor between its feet, without protest. Some owners have noticed that their *Nodosaurus* smiles at them from time to time. This eerie grin can be found in human babies after feeding, and the cause is the same (see Indigestion, p. 93).

    Nodosaurus is really very tender for an ankylosaur (personality, not meat). When you enter its quarters it will nuzzle you, probably hoping to get an extra bowl of sprouts, but will not show any disappointment if the food is foreign or raw; instead it will assume that you too have been let down by fate and often insist that you share some of the less appetizing food that it may have left for a later snack. It will pay you to be very tactful in this situation.

Feeding: As far as feeding is concerned, it is the hardest ankylosaur to please. However, the traditional British method of overboiling vegetables will usually convert even the hardest plant material to the appropriate mushy consistency.

Housing: See pages 64–5.

Breeding: See pages 64–5. *Nodosaurus* seems to have little interest in sex, with most males preferring to spend their evenings in quiet comtemplation of the floor. Many breeders now add aphrodisiacs to the normal feed. The most effective amatory aids seem to be figs, prunes and senna-pods: be prepared for the consequences.

Availability: There is at present a good supply of *Nodosaurus*, although you will probably need to go to cowboy country (the Olde Worlde Dino Shoppynge Centers of Kansas and Wyoming are best) to get really good specimens.

Left: Like Euoplocephalus *(p.70),* Nodosaurus *loves being taken on walks. Make sure you are equipped to clean up after your dinosaur.*

8 | DINOSAURS FOR ZOOS AND SAFARI PARKS

The dinosaurs that follow are suitable for keeping only under the excellent and professional conditions found in the larger zoos or, in some cases, safari parks. Private collectors should avoid them, particularly the carnivores: *Postosuchus*, despite of its tendency to kill people, is like a young lamb compared *Ceratosaurus*, let alone that cruel and legendary creature of science fact, *Tyrannosaurus*. On the other hand, the vegetarians, such as *Stegosaurus* and *Triceratops*, although easier to feed, are well beyond the competence of even the most enthusiastic amateur.

If you want to keep the bigger dinosaurs, you will need space: safari parks constructed in the grounds of stately homes can be ideal. Brontosaurs are the obvious starting point, but the intrepid entrepreneur will want to diversify into frilled dinosaurs and ostrich dinosaurs, and even take up the challenge of *Quetzalcoatlus* or the carnosaurs.

Brontosaurs

Most of the dinosaurs that can be used in safari parks are sauropods, popularly known as brontosaurs. However, more people have failed with brontosaurs, despite their familiar, long-necked, long-tailed appearance, than with any other group of dinosaurs. The main problem concerns their size: the sheer scale of the creatures is difficult to grasp. In addition, brontosaurs must live in herds to be happy, and they need lots of space. For this reason alone, if you keep brontosaurs I recommend you start with a relatively small one, such as *Massospondylus*. When you have succeeded with tiny animals only 4 metres (13 feet) long, you will be in a position to move on to bigger ones, such as *Dicraeosaurus*, before climaxing with giants such as *Diplodocus* and *Brachiosaurus*.

Keeping this brontosaur and displaying it to the public are feasible in the summer if you have 40 hectares (100 acres) or so of parkland with strong fencing. In the winter (except in the tropics), housing them and putting them on view are big problems, space and heat in particular. Of the methods attempted, converted airship hangars seem to have worked best, although millennium domes have been suggested. Brontosaurs are sufficiently sociable to need company indoors, so I cannot recommend individually heated pens. A lonely brontosaur becomes an unhealthy brontosaur. When all danger of frost has passed, you can keep it outside in its park or scrubland, provided it is well fenced. You will need stout metal palings. Although electric fencing is tempting and usually effective, on too many occasions the shocked twitch has broken the electric wire and allowed the entire herd to escape into the countryside. It must be added that the male *Dicraeosaurus*, the smallest brontosaur, is the only one likely to see a man as a possible predator, and to make a real effort to beat him flat. The keeper should be a woman or small man.

When your brontosaurs produce young, the herd organizes itself to protect them. In times of danger, whether real or not, the babies gather in a cluster and are surrounded by a ring of females. The males roam around the edge of the ring, trying to identify the source of danger and then charging at it in a comprehensive but uncomprehending way. This is dangerous because, although a male brontosaur doesn't usually associate a tiny man-sized figure with danger, it is quite likely to tread on him by mistake. Once brontosaurs learn to recognize someone, a process that may take some months, they will tolerate his (or, better still, her) presence among them, even close to the young, which can then be tended individually if necessary. After prolonged exposure, a herd of brontosaurs will become accustomed to people and even motor vehicles. However, there is still a high risk of cars being crushed by mistake and safari park managers must either run a securely fenced road through the enclosure or provide special crush-proof vehicles. A road should disappear into a tunnel from time to time so that the brontosaurs can cross freely above it.

The horned and frilled dinosaurs
The ceratopians, of which *Triceratops* is the best-known example, were the last dinosaurs to evolve.

It is a pity that, except for *Protoceratops* (p. 57) and *Leptoceratops* (p. 25), most of them are too big for the man in the street to keep. I know that *Triceratops* is tempting, but you should really leave it to those zoos that can give it plenty of space. All the ceratopians but *Leptoceratops* are quadrupeds. Of these, all but *Protoceratops* are very large quadrupeds. They have very big heads and beaks, and all of them have immense frills of bone protecting the neck and shoulders. Most of them have at least one long horn, and usually three, on their head. The sharp, horny beak, used to chop up food, can also be used to chop up enemies.

Because their brains are small it may take weeks or months to sort out their friends from their foes. For this reason alone the ceratopians need specially careful treatment: they can cause problems.

Carnosaurs
All the carnosaurs are carnivores and none has much discrimination in any way relevant to us. They are all bipedal; all have huge jaws supplied with horrid teeth; all have huge feet armed with horrid claws; all will kill and eat anything that moves; all have proved to be treacherous and fatal friends, even when hand-reared from the egg. I cannot recommend any of them as a pet, not even the smaller ones.

How can even big zoos cope with carnosaurs? There must be extremely secure centrally-heated pits and a capacity to supply the meat that will be needed. A useful rule of thumb for quantity is one duck per day per 3-metre (10-foot) length. For the larger carnosaurs you can start thinking in terms of geese, pigs, donkeys, horses, cattle, bison and so on. I recommend a routine of feast and fast, the fasts lasting for at least a week, and probably much longer.

Accidents are bound to happen, and with carnosaurs this will unfortunately mean fairly large-scale death and destruction. Keeping them in captivity is monumentally unwise. Unfortunately, carnosaurs have always attracted the crowds and there will always be those who are prepared to gamble human lives for money.

Dicraeosaurus

'Two-meat-tray Lizard', from Greek δι– *(two)* + κρειον *(meat-tray)* + σαυρος *(lizard). A reference to the amount of meat a hunter can expect to get as his share of a carcass: this dinosaur is a popular diet item in Tanzania.*

A realistic first brontosaur for your stately safari park: given sufficient space and housing it is easily kept and satisfactorily fertile if proper precautions are taken.

If you want to keep brontosaurs, I recommend that you start with *Dicraeosaurus*. At only 13 metres (43 feet) long and 3 metres (10 feet) high, it is the brontosaur with which you are most likely to succeed. It is the usual brontosaur shape, with tale held out stiffly to counterbalance the long neck. In colour it is brontosaur grey, the young being rather darker. As with all brontosaurs, its intelligence is negligible and its food vegetable.

You can keep the dung (indeed, you would be foolish not to) and use it to fertilize the summer feeding grounds. If you prefer, you can bag it and sell it at local farmers' markets. It is, for dinosaur dung, relatively inoffensive. *Dicraeosaurus* is a member of a notably brainless group of dinosaurs and has difficulty, it is fair to say, with all man-made objects. It will walk into walls, high-tension cables, street-lamps, fast-food stalls, cathedrals and so on: the damage caused by a

woman is best) to show her mettle by consoling the fearful creature, using gentle and soothing words and, wherever this is safe, friendly and reassuring caresses. When the brontosaur has recovered, it can be led home, gently and quietly, to the familiar safety of its own pasture and companions.

Feeding: Between 200 and 300 kilograms (440–660 pounds) of vegetation per *Dicraeosaurus* per day is needed: fortunately, most vegetable matter is accepted. Provide facilities for regular feeding at a height of from 2 to 7 metres (6 ½ to 22 feet) from the floor.

Housing: See the introduction to this chapter.

Breeding: Provided that a largish herd is kept with plenty of space (about 3 hectares/7 acres per female), eggs will be laid from time to time without any help being needed from you, the owner. Young hatch early in the summer and can run around actively after a few minutes.

Availability: Tendaguru Hill Farm Supplies in Tanzania.

Left: Watch out! That lawnmower might upset the Dicraeosaurus herd. (Note the rare sighting of Seismosaurus *just behind the house.)*

herd on the loose must be reckoned in six or seven figures and will have to be borne by you or your insurer.

You must also bear in mind the psychological, as well as physical, damage suffered by your dinosaurs. Life was much simpler in the late Jurassic. When something unexpected happened, it was nearly always best to stampede: this gave you a good chance of escaping the carnosaur, volcano, flash flood or whatever phenomenon had surprised you. So when your *Dicraeosaurus* sees a hot-air balloon, or trips over a barbed-wire fence, or hears a band playing, it runs, as quickly as it can, in a straight line. When it stops running it will be bewildered and unhappy: everything around it is new and strange. Now is the time for your brontoherd (a

Scelidosaurus

'ATROCIOUSLY WICKED LIZARD', from Latin sceleratus (wicked) + Greek σαυρος (lizard). It's not at all clear why this mild animal should be so described: I suspect the name is derived from the Roman Sceleratus Campus, the place where virgins who had broken their vows were, quite properly, entombed alive.

Although generally unpopular and a fussy eater, it is a safer, though less spectacular, dinosaur than *Stegosaurus* (p. 79), and should be tried first.

Although palaeontologists now believe that *Scelidosaurus* is essentially an ankylosaur, the more realist dinosaur-keeper thinks of it as a stegosaur, and, as such, difficult to feed and rather fussy as to temperature; its temper is uncertain and its reactions often delayed to the point of inertia. But *Scelidosaurus* has a small and dedicated following: if you own a zoo that must have a stegosaur, *Scelidosaurus* is the one to start with. At 4 metres (13 feet) long and less than 150 kilograms (332 pounds) in weight, it is more manageable and less delicate than other stegosaurs. Furthermore, it does not often inflict gross damage on its keepers. Sadly, for these reasons, the dedicated stegosaurophile is usually less interested in *Scelidosaurus* than in the others, preferring the grotesque unpredictability of the better-known *Stegosaurus*.

Scelidosaurus is covered by small bony plates embedded in the skin. Some of these are very complicated in shape. It has triangular spikes along the middle of its neck, over its hips and down its tail. Although I have suggested that it is an unpopular dinosaur, I hope I haven't put you off obtaining one: it is finicky with its food, true, but eats less than the other stegosaurs; it needs to be kept warm, certainly, but its smaller size allows you to use a smaller cage; I don't deny that it is stupid and may lash out unexpectedly with its tail, but the usual result is a

severe bruising or, at worst, a broken leg. Although *Scelidosaurus* is eminently suitable for zoos, you must remember that most zoos are in cities and that the air in many cities is polluted. Polluted air elicits bronchitis; so may poor living conditions, especially cold and damp ones. The symptoms and cure are the same as for asthma (see p. 92). Heated Stegosaur Houses are the answer.

Feeding: I must warn you that all the stegosaurs (and in this respect *Scelidosaurus* behaves like a stegosaur) are difficult to feed. Naturally herbivorous, *Scelidosaurus* is rather a fussy eater, liking soft vegetables and fruit, but not grass. If you have good access to horsetails, your problems are over. Some owners – not many – have succeeded with marestails; some zoos have succeeded with grain. As grain-eaters swallow their food whole, they need plenty of grit. Charcoal should be added to grit in the ratio 1:20 to ward off flatulence. Automatic seed-hoppers will save labour.

Housing: It needs to be kept warm: use a heated enclosure.

Breeding: Not yet achieved.

Availability: There are shops in South Dorset, in the Charmouth area, where you will be able to get an address of a supplier. By no means cheap.

Stegosaurus

An unintended spoonerism of Stesagorus, son of Cymon, the half-brother of Miltiades (son of Cypselus).

Suitable for the well-appointed zoo that has already succeeded with *Scelidosaurus*. Difficult, delicate and spectacular; sure to draw the crowds. Not for the private collector.

This dinosaur is 8 metres (26 feet) long and over 2 tons in weight. A series of triangular bony plates is attached to the skin of the back. At the end of the tail are two pairs of spikes, as in *Kentrosaurus* (p. 63). It is a spectacular creature, the idea of which, like the idea of *Tyrannosaurus* (p. 90), is beloved by children; it is a shame that so few zoos seem able to keep them.

Stegosaurus has an almost unique thermo-regulation device. The bony plates on its back are covered with skin and are well supplied with blood vessels. When the animal is too hot, the plates stand up vertically on its back and the blood supply to their surfaces is increased. In this way, heat is carried away from the body to the plates, where it radiates away, cooling the stegosaur. The broadest part of the plate is not nearest the base but about a third of the way up, so that the most effective cooling is some way from the body. Also, the plates are not opposite one another, but alternate left and right, allowing air currents to flow between. When the weather is cold, *Stegosaurus* lays the plates flat on their sides on its sides and cuts down the blood supply, so that the heat is lost far more slowly. When *Stegosaurus* is cooler than the outside world, perhaps when it wakes up in the morning, the dorsal plates absorb heat from the sun. This allows it to wander about in cool weather and live in latitudes other stegosaurs cannot reach.

Feeding: *Stegosaurus* has two dozen small teeth on each side of the jaw and cannot eat hard food. However, most individuals can be weaned from their preferred horsetails and cycads to other foods. Try deciduous leaves, cow-cake, silage and cabbage. The leaves of beet, carrot, turnip and some orchids (such as *Vanilla*) can be offered when appropriate.

Housing: *Stegosaurus* is the ultimate stegosaur, as you would expect. It needs heated winter quarters

and a cosy dwelling for summer nights. Its great size allows it to put up with a great deal of cold weather, although it draws the line at frost. They must, of course, be securely enclosed, while being permitted plenty of sunlight. Nonetheless, I should not care to take on the husbandry of *Stegosaurus*, unless I had the sort of fortified swamp that I recommend for the smaller *Kentrosaurus* (p. 63).

Breeding: Great success has been reported from Quarry 13 in Albany County, Wyoming, and in Quarry 1 in Fremont County, Colorado.

Availability: As well as young, captive-bred specimens in Quarries 1 and 13 above, specimens can be obtained from Salt Lake Stegos in Utah and the Rogers Stegoshop in Oklahoma.

Triceratops

'THREE HORNS IDEA', from Greek τρεις (three) + κέρας (horn) + ὄψίς (vision). The composer Sergei Prokofiev, wondering what to use to represent the wolf in his 'Peter and the Wolf', happened to see a herd of Triceratops grazing in Moscow Zoo, and was inspired to choose three horns.

To the zoo with wide open spaces big enough for a herd, *Triceratops* will bring all the atmosphere of the Wyoming Upper Cretaceous.

The beautiful proportions of *Triceratops* may prevent you from appreciating the sheer size of the creature at first. You will be tempted to think of it as a sort of rhinoceros; but a big male is 9 metres (30 feet) long and weighs 6 tons, twice the length and three times the weight of a rhino!

The head seems to make up a third of the total length, but most of this is not really part of the true head. A great frill of bone projects from the skull back over the neck nearly to the shoulders. As well as being a useful shield against other males and predators such as *Tyrannosaurus*, this bone acts as an attachment area for the enormous muscles of the jaws and neck. Two large horns stick out over the eyes, and another over the nose.

Although you can keep *Triceratops* in small groups, or even singly, it cannot be denied that it will really flourish only in a largish herd. In such a group, the genetic Herd Dominance Hierarchy (HDH) manifests itself and the keeper's personal relationships with individual ceratopians, difficult at the best of times, becomes submerged by the various Innate Herd-Structure Maintenance Behaviours (IHSMBs). To put it more simply, if a male dinosaur thinks that you are another male dinosaur, the HDH part of the IHSMB will preponderate and may, by a process of social facilitation, self-propagate. Every organism ecphorizes the inherited engram of its origin: as a result, you may find two dozen six-ton animals galloping at you head down, metre-long horns foremost, at 50 kilometres (31 miles) per hour.

As you might have gathered, the males fight each other in spring and early summer, which is their mating season. Rivals face each other, bellowing and alternately bowing and tossing their massive heads, showing their opponents their horns and (often brightly coloured) shields. Usually, matters proceed no further, because the smaller or weaker male moves off. But if the two are evenly matched, they will fight, locking horns or ramming each other. These battles may result in severe wounds, but deaths are rare.

With individual specimens of *Triceratops* some form of mutual affection can build up. It is not an intelligent dinosaur and it may well mistake you for somebody else. As it is big, bulky and beaked, the result may be irreversible.

Feeding: Its jaws contain neat and narrow rows of numerous teeth, which work like scissors, and it has a strong and sharp horny beak. With this formidable feeding apparatus, *Triceratops* can deal with almost any vegetable material and prefers fibrous and juicy plants, such as young palms and giant rhubarb. Plant its enclosures with staple foods, such as giant redwoods, maidenhair trees, poplars, oaks and maples. You must make very large quantities available.

Housing: Several kilohectares of parkland containing the plants mentioned above, surrounded by a moat bounded by a high stone wall, with heated, covered areas for cold weather. A converted airfield, with hangars, is a good basis from which to start.

Breeding: Leave them to it.

Availability: Green Mountain Creek Cresteds, Denver, Colorado and the chain of Tricerashops in Niobrara County, Wyoming will give you the greatest choice, but the Red Deer River Retailers in Canada, as well as outlets in Montana and South Dakota are useful sources.

Struthiomimus

'SPARROW FARCE', from Greek στρουθίον *(sparrow)*
+ Latin mimus *(farce), referring to its habit of early rising.*

An extremely fast, two-legged
runner, *Struthiomimus* really
needs the wide open spaces
provided by a park. Easily
fed and cared for. No
landed gentry should
be without a herd.

Struthiomimus is a very ostrich-like dinosaur, with
a toothless, horny beak. With its long tail stiffened
as a counterbalance to its long neck, it is vey like
Ornithomimus (p. 39), but has longer arms and
heavier claws at the end of its fingers.

If you have kept *Ornithomimus* and been charmed,
Struthiomimus offers an extension of the experience.
No larger than *Ornithomimus*, *Struthiomimus* is
faster on the straight (up to 80 kilometres/50 miles
per hour) and should be ridden only by those who
have completely mastered *Ornithomimus*.

If it has enough space, it will develop its
own social organization, the herd having its own
recognized pecking order. This social structure is
relatively rigid and family groups soon separate out
after some initial sparring between the bigger males.
The family sticks together as a sub-group within the
herd, with the father as dominant animal. Curiously
enough, in the herd as a whole the leader, or
dominant dinosaur, is as often as not a female
– usually a widow, but rarely an old maid.

Harmless to tourists.

Feeding: Its diet is similar to that of *Ornithomimus*,
but it is much more herbivorous: eggs, fruit,
branches. In fact, its diet is much like that of the
ostrich and very little is refused. Give it a small
mammal or a lizard for a treat.

Housing: It needs to be kept in herds to flourish
and, as you can appreciate, needs enclosures of
several hectares in area.

Breeding: Pairs form naturally in the herd and eggs
are laid in scrapes in the ground. They will hatch if
the herd is left to its own devices.

Availability: Red Deer River Retailers, Alberta is the
best, but you can pick up nice American specimens in
New Jersey.

Postosuchus

'How-d'you-mean-Croc', from Greek πως (in what way), + τω (in this case) + σουχος (crocodile), from the Famous Last Words of its discoverer.

Not a suitable dinosaur for the amateur; unpredictable, active, predatory and cannibalistic. Do not be tempted by the chicks!

At 6 metres (20 feet) long, *Postosuchus* is really a bigger and more horrible version of *Euparkeria* (p. 16), although it still walks and runs on all four feet. Its back and sides are covered by bony plates; the head is deep and the very powerful jaws are full of sharp teeth.

Young ones are fairly manageable; a zoo planning to keep more than one in the same enclosure should make sure they are the same size. Not for nothing are they protected by bony plates: they are very likely to kill and eat smaller and weaker companions, as cannibalism doesn't worry them in the slightest. Because they have a good turn of speed, they do pose a threat to life and limb. The smaller species, are fairly easy to handle, but not to be trusted; the female of the species is more deadly than the male.

Two ailments in particular afflict *Postosuchus*: roup and croup (see pp. 92–3).

Feeding: *Postosuchus* is a highly predatory carnivore: it needs plenty of meat in large chunks. It is, unexpectedly, fond of birds, and the bigger they are the better: give it ostriches, cassowaries and so on.

Housing: Keep them permanently behind bars or enclosed with (strong) wire netting, surrounded by a moat.

Breeding: *Postosuchus* can be bred. Eggs are laid in a crude nest in sand or light earth. They are scarcely buried and the female stays near the site to defend the nest against other *Postosuchus* and also Man. When the chicks hatch, she protects them for a while, then loses maternal interest. After a few days she regains interest, although this is now gastronomic, and she will eat her babies if she comes across them. Better to collect them and rear them yourself.

Availability: Arizona is the place for *Postosuchus*. Try catching your own in the Petrified Forest. Alternatively, many a shop in St. John's will offer to find one for you, or you can mail order one from Post Quarry Postosuchians by Post in Texas.

Ceratosaurus

'HORNY LIZARD', from Greek κέρατινος (horny) + Greek σαυρος (lizard), from the male's uninhibited courtship activity.

If your zoo needs a carnosaur, *Ceratosaurus*, one of the smallest of them, is the one to choose. It is beyond the scope of even the biggest private collectors (outside America).

Ceratosaurus is distinguished by a bony spike on its snout and a bony knob above each eye. These are used, as we shall see later, in battles of sexual rivalry between males.

Feeding: Two ducks a day is enough for a fully grown male. For reasons of conservation, I cannot really recommend the eggs of other dinosaurs, but there is no doubt that *Ceratosaurus* does particularly appreciate the addition of eggs to its diet, so very large numbers of birds' eggs should be used; ostrich eggs are best, followed by cassowary, but chickens' eggs are the cheapest. Perhaps, as a birthday treat, you could give them *Protoceratops* eggs.

Housing: See under 'Carnosaurs' (p. 75). They must be kept singly. Even if you keep a few females together, sooner or later one will be killed and eaten by its companions, then another and so on, until only one remains.

Breeding: Males fight one another. In the wild, such sexual sparring is ritualized into a head-butting routine in which neither of the contestants is seriously hurt. When one of the rivals recognizes the superior strength of his opponent he stops the butting and runs away. The winner, no longer stimulated to attack by the sight of another male, ignores the loser. Do not be misled by this into thinking that you can keep two males in one pit. The vanquished one, prevented from escape by the walls of the pit, is unable to avoid the victor, who will attack him without mercy, not only with the top of his head but also with tooth and claw. There can be only one outcome: the death of a dinosaur. You may be tempted to keep a pair together, hoping for the arrival of eggs. Resist temptation: a male will kill a female, not out of malice, but through insistent and violent courtship. Allow them to meet each other once, and then hope for the best. If eggs result, incubate them artificially – if you can get hold of them.

Availability: The traditional source in Fremont County, Colorado has been displaced by the Carnosauction House in the Cleveland-Lloyd Quarry, Utah, now a designated national landmark.

Apatosaurus

'Bastard Lizard', from Greek ἀπάτωρ (fatherless) + σαυρος (lizard), from the difficulty in establishing paternity, owing to the informal nature of their mating behaviour.

For an enormous enclosed area, the most brontosaurian dinosaur of all. With a lake in summer and warmth in winter, a herd will give you an enviable reputation.

Apatosaurus is as typical a brontosaur as you can get, with a tiny head, a long neck and a long tail. It will draw the crowds as well as any other brontosaur, apart from the elegant *Diplodocus* and, of course, the giant *Brachiosaurus*. Buns, ice-creams and most of the other food that children throw out of cars will not harm it. Treat it with respect, just as you would any other brontosaur.

If you have an emergency involving a member of the viewing public – say *Apatosaurus* picks a child up by the collar – you can play on the brontosaur's immense gullibility to retrieve the situation. At the sight of a large carnosaur (*Tyrannosaurus* is ideal) they will drop everything and run. Even though they never encounter *Tyrannosaurus* in the wild, they sense danger. Fortunately, you do not need a real *Tyrannosaurus* to frighten a brontosaur: keep a lifesize model at the ready (an inflatable will do, either inflated or self-inflating) and wheel it into view as soon as the crisis occurs. Your insurance company will appreciate this.

Feeding: As *Dicraeosaurus* (p. 77), but more.

Housing: As well as at least 30 hectares (75 acres) of parkland and scrub, a substantial lake must be provided for mating. The same precautions must be taken when admitting the public as for all brontosaurs. In winter, warmth is needed: you will need an enormous enclosed area of the type I have described under 'Brontosaurs' (p.74–5).

Breeding: Being 21 metres (69 feet) long, *Apatosaurus* finds copulation difficult under normal gravitational conditions; the problem is solved by the buoyancy provided by water. The males and females splash into the water together, usually in large numbers. They are competent swimmers and the sight of all their companions splashing around them stimulates them and provokes them to pre-coital activity, or 'courtship', as romantics call it. Mating in brontosaurs is more prosaic than poetic, although there is an epic quality. Although the possession of a penis helps, copulation is still difficult. Many hours of 30-ton gambollings and stentorian bellowings by the male must pass before the female is convinced that it is a good idea to respond, by coiling her neck and tail around his. When this stage is reached, coitus is a formality. Like other formal occasions, it may last a long time, but is usually over by sundown. Passion wanes as the day cools. Ten or so oval eggs are laid in spring.

Availability: The Morrison Brontobooth in Colorado is always a sound source; in Wyoming, the Como Bluff Brontocenter is probably just as good, but the nearby Bone Cabin Quarry has a reputation for careless identification: caveat emptor! Otherwise, the usual outlets in Oklahoma and Utah shouldn't disappoint you.

Massospondylus

'STICKY MUSSEL', from Latin massa *(that which adheres together like dough) + Greek* σφονδυλος *(mussel): referring to the appearance of a persistently amatory mating pair.*

This elegant prosauropod is an impressive inhabitant of any safari park, where it is easily fed and accommodated; gentle, but too big to wander among pedestrians.

At 4 metres (13 feet) long, *Massospondylus* approaches the sort of size on which the reputation of dinosaurs largely rests. It is popular with safari park owners and visitors, since it is so friendly. It will lumber up to cars and peer through the windows. This is perfectly safe, as long as the windows are kept closed, and provides excellent opportunities for home movie enthusiasts. If you find one in the middle of the road, you may be in for a long wait: it is not deaf, simply unmoved by the sound of car horns. Just sit tight, get your camera ready and wait until the line of traffic reaches back to the park entrance: a game warden will arrive and move the animal by offering it roses.

Feeding: *Massospondylus* is essentially a vegetarian and not expensive to maintain, in summer, anyway. It likes rose bushes best – this can be a nuisance – but many individuals will adapt fairly happily to brambles.
Housing: Unlike its bigger relations, *Massospondylus* doesn't need the open spaces of a safari park, though it will flourish in them. It will be happy kept outside in a roomy paddock. Bring it in winter, of course.
Breeding: No information is available; maintain your stock by bringing in new specimens from suppliers.
Availability: Zimbabwe Zoo Supplies and the South African travelling Dinosaur Kiosks are the best sources, but you can get fair specimens in parts of Arizona.

Camarasaurus

'VAULT LIZARD', from Greek καμάρά *(vault) +* σαυρος *(lizard). This refers to the use of the young as vaulting horses in the more old-fashioned circuses.*

Delightful, charming and full of character. Ideal material for someone moving into brontosaur-husbandry who has already cut his teeth on *Dicraeosaurus*.

Of all the brontosaurs, *Camarasaurus* is the one you could most truly say possessed a character. Some describe the babies as 'delightful' and 'charming', and so they are. But they grow up, and with maturity comes a psychological need for the herd. When they are kept in a herd, their charm and individuality tend to be submerged in the group's collective unconscious. But kept alone, they pine and wane.

However, if you can manage to extricate two or three very young (three to four weeks old) *Camarasaurus* from the herd and exhibit them in a small paddock, you will draw huge crowds of children and their parents, who will find the creatures' playful fighting and the squeaky noises

they make highly amusing. Surround the paddock with souvenir shops, refreshment halls, beer tents, merry-go-rounds and craft stalls. Detaching the young from the herd is best accomplished by a skilful lasso-artist working from an armoured car. Return the young to the herd before they are two months old.
Feeding, Housing and Breeding: See *Dicraeosaurus* (p. 77)
Availability: The best specimens come from the Carnegie Museum shop at Dinosaur National Monument, Utah, but less perfect specimens can be obtained from Canyon City Camarasaurs, Colorado and Como Bluff Brontocenter, Wyoming. Otherwise, the usual outlets in Oklahoma.

Diplodocus

'DOUBLE BEAM', from Greek διπλοος (double) + δοκός (beam); this refers to the great width of this dinosaur.

This is one of the longest dinosaurs, a graceful brontosaur for the connoisseur. Try one when you have succeeded with the others, but not until then.

Although *Diplodocus* is, at 27 metres (89 feet), a very long dinosaur, 13 of those metres (43 feet) are tail and 8 metres (26 feet) are neck. It is a slender brontosaur and has a thumb-claw for mating and, on occasion, defence. I don't think it is stretching affection too far to describe it as graceful, even delicately beautiful. It is particularly suitable for the upper end of the safari park market: those parks that were landscaped centuries ago by a capable master. Here the visitor, emerging from an ancient stand of oak or beech, is presented with a vista that uplifts his (or perhaps her) careworn twenty-first-century heart: perhaps magnolia and rhododendron in the foreground, a rolling lawn, a lake (with a discreet waterfall), some elegant cedars strewn here and there, some thistle-filled meadows and a distant arboraceous hillside, a scene, you might think, impossible to enhance. But a herd of *Diplodocus*, quietly browsing in the middle distance, adds something difficult to define but real and powerful: it has to do with the fourth dimension, that of time. The realization that these noble creatures have been living their innocent pastoral lives in such a place and in such a manner for 190 million years gives the twenty-first-century visitor an insight, at the same time humbling and uplifting, into the essential unchangeability of life on Earth.

Treat *Diplodocus* like other brontosaurs, but make allowances: it is dim-witted, even by the standards of other brontosaurs. Fragile, beautiful and stupid: a combination that has appealed to Man since Adam.

It also produces immense amounts of dung, which you can sell either to farmers and garden centres as manure, or to artists, who are becoming increasingly excited by its potential as a semi-temporary material for sculpture and other forms of plastic art.

Feeding: See *Dicraeosaurus* (p. 77).

Housing: See *Dicraeosaurus* (p. 77).

Breeding: See *Dicraeosaurus* (p. 77). The thumb-claw is used to cling on to the female while mating: it is certainly worth standing clear on these occasions.

Availability: You may pick one up at the ranch of M.P. Felch, near Canyon City in Colorado, but you're more likely to be lucky in Sheep Creek, Albany County, Wyoming. Otherwise, you'll have to rely on the usual outlets in Montana and Utah.

Right: Thrill your compy with a surprise trip to the safari park to meet some of his (or her) larger relatives.

Brachiosaurus

'SHORT LIZARD', from Greek βραχύς *(short)* + σαυρος *(lizard),
a curious name for the tallest of the dinosaurs.*

As one of the largest land animals in the world, this is the Everest of dinosaur-keeping. Problems abound, but it is a challenge that the bravest will want to accept.

Up to now, *Brachiosaurus*, at 23 metres (75 feet) in length and 50 or more tons in weight (the weight of sixteen elephants), has always been considered the largest dinosaur, although television advertisements for '*Supersaurus*', '*Ultrasaurus*' and '*Seismosaurus*' in the Colorado area show us that big dinosaurs are being heavily promoted these days. It is not the usual brontosaur shape, as its front legs are much longer than its hind ones, and is thus the most upright of the brontosaurs: with neck stretched up it can be up to 12 metres (39 feet) high. Its head has a distinguished, even aristocratic look, with nostrils on the top in a little lump. Its tail is relatively short, of course, in obedience to the Principle of Moments. It is an awesome animal and, if you succeed with it, your name will become household and your herd of dinosaurs a living legend.

Some safari park owners are experimenting with 'Brach-rides'; this is a controversial area at the moment, because, although *Brachiosaurus* is gentle, it does lack that intellectual rigour that is so important when carrying large numbers of people on your back.

Feeding: As *Dicraeosaurus* (p. 77), but much more food needed.

Housing: Most brontosaur winter quarters pose immense problems: those of *Brachiosaurus* pose immense problems, even to those dinosaur-keepers who have solved the problems posed by the other brontosaurs. If you are looking for a crumb of comfort, you may find it in the fact that a large lake is not strictly needed by *Brachiosaurus*. A pond of about a hectare or two (2–5 acres) will be enough for the summer; a heated, running stream, say 2 metres (6 ½ feet) wide and 2 metres (6 ½ feet) deep, flowing through the winter quarters should help tide the herd over the dark months of winter. If you are serious, there are now companies (e.g. Hercules Labor Inc.) that will arrange a system of sluices and dams to divert this stream over the floor to help clean the house (the so-called Augean Method).

Breeding: *Brachiosaurus* is by no means as easy to breed as some of the other brontosaurs. Try simulated rain to bring both sexes into heat.

Availability: The best outlets are Grand River Valley Dino Depot, in western Colorado and Tendaguru Hill Farm Supplies in Tanzania. Some noble families have struck it lucky in Algeria.

Quetzalcoatlus

'MONEY SNAKE', from quetzal *(the basic monetary unit of Guatemala)* + Nahuatl coatl *(serpent), referring to the immense cost of obtaining and keeping this animal.*

The largest flying animal, easily fed but not so easily housed. A drive-through desert safari park could be modified, at some expense, to display this majestic pterosaur.

Because it is a pterosaur, I should really place *Quetzalcoatlus* under 'Flying Pets' (p. 28), but its great size makes it suitable only for a very large safari park. With a wing span of up to 15 metres (49 feet), it dwarfs even *Pteranodon* (p. 29). It is as delicate in build as *Pteranodon*, too, but unlike *Pteranodon*, it is not covered with white fur. It will certainly attract the crowds. Remind them to bring binoculars!

Also unlike *Pteranodon*, *Quetzalcoatlus* will survive for years in captivity, although it doesn't really flourish. It relies on thermal currents to keep it aloft and needs to be kept in hot deserts where such vertical winds are common. Horizontal winds are another matter and can be dangerous to such a delicately built creature. In hot, windless weather it can be seen (don't forget your binoculars) soaring high in the sky, wheeling and circling with effortless grace, scanning the ground for food. It's probably best not to sunbathe or fall asleep in the enclosure.

Feeding: Its food is fish and other small animals: you should have plenty of animals available for it. In the first edition I suggested carrion, but it turns out that most *Quetzalcoatlus* will eat only living or freshly dead food. Your feeding regime should steer between surfeit and starvation: feed it when it begins to fly above naked eyesight.

Housing: It is clear that only a few safari parks will be suitable and these only for some of the time. What are the characteristics of a park suitable for *Quetzalcoatlus*? First, it must be situated in a hot desert; second, the desert must be windless. It need not be hot all the time, nor windless all the time, but there should be enough sun to produce the thermals needed to support the gliding *Quetzalcoatlus* and enough windless days for tourists to have a good chance of seeing it soaring above their heads without risking damage from unexpected gusts. For a safari park to justify its description the animals in it must be free-ranging, at least within their enclosure:

onlookers need to enter the enclosure in order to view them. A *Quetzalcoatlus* in a cage puts all heaven in a rage. But if it's allowed to fly, how can you prevent the escape of your pterosaur?

The best, perhaps the only, way is to build a high 'cage' around a site of at least 50 hectares (125 acres), although 250 hectares (620 acres) would be better. Nylon netting attached firmly to the ground and held taut at the other end by helium-filled balloons is the cheapest option. Check the netting regularly for signs of *Quetzalcoatlus* trying to escape. A height of 3,000–4,000 metres (10,000–13,000 feet) should be sufficient. Although it may soar higher than this in the wild, if you feed it well it doesn't need to fly high, preferring to hang up somewhere, upside-down in typical pterosaur fashion.

Breeding: Not yet accomplished, so prices are likely to be, like the animal, usually very high.

Availability: Big Bend Big Birds, in Texas, has a virtual monopoly on specimens.

Tyrannosaurus

'TYRANT LIZARD', from Greek τύραννος *(absolute monarch, sovereign, lord, master, tyrant)* + *Greek* σαυρος *(lizard), which just about says it all.*

The ultimate animal for the zoo with dwindling attendances. Literally awful and almost certainly needing a special insurance policy. By far the least suitable dinosaur to keep.

With *Tyrannosaurus* we reach the end of the line: with the possible exception of *Giganotosaurus*, it is the biggest and most formidable of the carnivorous dinosaurs. At 13 metres (43 feet) long, 5.5 metres (18 feet) high and weighing up to 7 tons, *Tyrannosaurus* is a machine for killing dinosaurs. Its head is 1.25 metres (4 feet) long and holds a battery of saw-edged teeth 15 centimetres (6 inches) long. Its main weapons are the huge hind feet, which bear talons 20 centimetres (8 inches) long. Its front legs are tiny and not used in catching or killing its prey: they are used to help *Tyrannosaurus* get up when it has been lying down. They are supported by massive shoulder muscles. It uses its claws as toothpicks and sexual aids.

Tyrannosaurus usually walks slowly and ponderously with its body held horizontally and in what has been described as a swan-neck curve for flexibility. The surprisingly short, but stiff and heavy, tail is raised off the ground and used as a counterweight. Although it seems clumsy and pigeon-toed, it is capable of moving more quickly in short bursts.

Feeding: See under 'Carnosaurs' (p. 75). James Farlow has calculated that it would take 292 lawyers, each weighing 68 kilograms (150 pounds), to keep a 4.5-ton *Tyrannosaurus* fed for a year, an understandably optimistic calculation.

Housing: See under 'Carnosaurs' (p. 75). You need to remember the particular problems involved in the management of 13-metre- (43-foot-) long carnivorous dinosaurs: space, feeding and insurance. For maximum security and minimum premiums, I suggest that around your *Tyrannosaurus* pit you build something similar to a maximum-security prison wall and that you keep watch around the clock; equip your sentries with searchlights and rockets. The public can view from the top of such a wall and from walkways suspended high above the

pit. Cage in all viewing points or your zoo will almost certainly be the scene of some spectacular homicides.

Breeding: The first edition of this book stated that 'it is only when kept in flocks that *Tyrannosaurus* will breed'. Exigencies of space and time just before publication meant that the words 'of sheep and herds of cattle', which should have followed 'flocks', were left out. My apologies to the unfortunately numerous zoos who lost so many of their expensive exhibits. In fact, both sexes are solitary, except for a very brief period of mating. The eggs are laid in a nest and covered with rotting vegetation for incubation. The young are about a metre (3 feet) long at birth and weigh about 6 kilograms (13 pounds). But do think before you take a baby home with you: will it be quite as cuddly in a year's time?

Availability: The Hell Creek KT Dinosaur Interface Emporium in Montana is the first and best source, but you can get them at TeeRex Supplies in Texas and Wyoming, as well as the usual Canadian auction rooms. The Mongolian Carnosaur Market is beginning to flourish, in spite of problems with the Ulan Bator horse breeders.

Right: A picture taken mere seconds before tragedy struck...

Ailments and Cures

Antibiotics
Not an ailment as such, but too often resorted to too quickly as a treatment. If your dinosaur is off-colour, it is important that you don't give it antibiotics, because these will kill the important intestinal flora. Prevention is better than cure: anticipate any health problems. At the first signs of ill-health, check your animals' diet, housing and all features of their environment that may be the cause. Only give antibiotics to herbivorous dinosaurs as a last resort and when prescribed by a qualified dinosaur vet. On the other hand, carnivores such as *Tyrannosaurus* respond very well to antibiotics, although there are often problems in administering them.

Asthma
Symptoms: Noisy and heavy breathing.
Cause: Mental: often caused by the need to make a decision. Mainly afflicts the bone-headed dinosaurs.
Treatment: Remove the cause (e.g. make all the dinosaur's decisions for it). If it seems chronic, try the Heat Treatment (see One-eyed Cold).

Cold
Symptoms: Unusual behaviour pattern, e.g. shivering, vertical jumping.
Cause: Dinosaur, particularly feet, allowed to get too cold.
Treatment: Keep its feet warm. Swab the throat with eucalyptus.

Constipation
Symptoms: Difficulty in passing droppings.
Cause: Not enough grit in the diet.
Treatment: More grit in the diet may be needed, but you can usually cure constipation by giving extra greens and fruits. If the problem seems immoveable, try that grand and traditional remedy, cod liver oil, either mixed with food or, in acutely costive cases, squirted straight into the mouth with a modified fire extinguisher.

Above all, remember that wood charcoal is necessary for all dinosaurs in captivity to absorb gases in the intestine and ward off flatulence, often a nuisance to the owners of the larger species.

Croup (*See* Roup)

Crooked Legs
Symptoms: Weak or crooked legs, particularly in the young.
Cause: This may be due to a deficiency of Calcium (Ca) and Vitamin D (calciferol).
Treatment: Add cod liver oil to the diet and make sure there is plenty of fresh green food available.

Depluming Scabies
Symptoms: Dinosaur tears its feathers out.
Cause: Mites irritating the skin.
Treatment: Dip the infected animal in a solution of 55 g (2 oz) soft soap and 55 g (2 oz) flowers of sulphate in 4.5 l (1 gal) of water at 38°C (100°F), then let it dry in a warm room. Spray the living quarters (the animal's) with creosote and air them.

Diarrhoea (*See* Enteritis)

Dyspepsia
Symptoms: Constipation.
Cause: Too little grit in the diet.
Treatment: Provide more grit.

Enteritis
Symptoms: Enteritis, in spite of appearances, is not to be confused with diarrhoea: dinosaur diarrhoea is actually inflammation of the enteric mucous membranes. Be that as it may, the symptoms are much the same: the droppings are very fluid, copious and green-tinted; they are always foul-smelling. The sick animal has a poor appetite and excessive thirst.
Cause: Probably dietary.
Treatment: Take the animal into a warm, even temperature of 29°C (84°F). If the skin is fouled, use a gentle jet hose to wash with disinfectant and water (take care!). Do not forget the feet and legs, and clean the vent with a soft brush (take great care!). Observe strict hygiene. For one week add 506 g (18 oz) powdered catachu, 13 g (1/2 oz) powdered calcium phenol sulphate, 13 g (1/2 oz) powdered sodium phenol sulphate, and 25 g (1 oz) powdered zinc sulphate to every litre (2 pints) of drinking water. If you find it hard to raise the temperature of its living quarters, use a hospital cage: you will need a box cage with an armoured glass front, which can be artificially heated.

Hard-shelled Eggs
Symptoms: Eggs are surprisingly heavy and the shells opaque.
Cause: Insufficient humidity.
Treatment: Moisten the eggs daily (twice daily in low humidity) with warm water.

Impaction of the Crop
Symptoms: Constant belching; the observant hand may be able to feel a tell-tale lump in the throat.
Cause: In free-range dinosaurs, coarse vegetation, hair, feathers or plastic bags prevent food from entering the stomach.
Treatment: The best thing to do is inject antiseptic soda-water, from a syphon, into the throat, or thump the dinosaur's back with a padded caber. If these measures fail, you may have to think of medication.

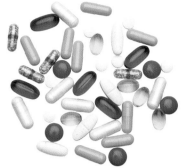

Indigestion
Symptoms: Dyspepsia and flatulence.
Cause: Too little grit in diet.
Treatment: Provide more grit in diet.

Juvenile Crooked Legs (*See* Juvenile Weak Legs)

Juvenile Weak Legs
Symptoms: Young with weak or crooked legs.
Cause: Deficiency of Calcium (Ca) and Vitamin D (calciferol).
Treatment: Add cod liver oil to the diet and make sure there is plenty of fresh green food available.

Lameness (*See* Partial Paralysis)

Locomotor Ataxia
Symptoms: The animal performs uncontrolled movements and presents a drunken appearance.
Cause: A genetic disease.
Treatment: Incurable.

One-eyed Cold
Symptoms: The frequent closing of one eye.
Cause: Dinosaur allowed to get too cold.
Treatment: Isolate immediately and try the Heat Treatment (see Enteritis) first. If this fails, try the treatment for Cold; if this fails, try, in order, the treatments for Croup, Juvenile Weak Legs and Partial Paralysis. If all these treatments fail, the probability is that your dinosaur may have to be put down by a qualified Dinosaur Vet (in the USA, a qualified Dinosaur Veterinarian); in countries bordering the Mediterranean Sea, the local butcher will usually oblige.

Partial Paralysis
Symptoms: Partial paralysis.
Cause: Deficiency of Vitamin D or lime.
Treatment: More calcium in diet, or Vitamin tablets (this may involve expensive quantities in the case of the larger dinosaurs). If this fails, try massaging legs (and wings in the case of flying animals) with methylated spirit.

Roup

Ordinary Roup
Symptoms: Mucus gathers in the mouth.
Cause: Overcrowding and bad ventilation.
Treatment: A mild antiseptic can cure ordinary roup.

Diphtheric Roup
Symptoms: This is the more serious kind of roup, in which a yellow deposit forms in the back of the throat and the dinosaur frequently sneezes.
Cause: Overcrowding and bad ventilation.
Treatment: A mild antiseptic may help; if you catch it early enough, diphtheric roup may be cured by iodine, glycerol and balsam, as in Stegosaur Pox.

Croup
Croup is either a complication of roup or caused by wounds from fighting. It is very contagious and the best remedy is total destruction.

Soft-shelled Eggs
Symptoms: Eggs have soft shells.
Cause: May be caused by nervous shock, but probably due to a deficiency of calcium in the mother's diet.
Treatment: Add lime to her food.

Stegosaur Pox
Symptoms: This presents as scabs, lesions of the mouth and nose, a discharge from the mouth and difficulty in breathing. The dinosaur goes off its feed and looks ill, with drooping tail and back-spikes.
Cause: Contact with infected animal.
Treatment: Treat the scabs three times daily with a solution of equal parts of iodine, glycerol and Friar's Balsam. This requires immense care and I suggest the use of an accurate and easily aimed long-range spray. Most modern fire brigades have efficient means of disseminating liquids and would, I am sure, be happy to advise. If they are unco-operative, you can easily adapt a foam-based wasp-killer, obtainable at all good hardware stores.

Weak Legs (*See* Crooked Legs)

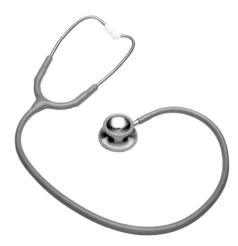

Classification
How your dinosaurs are related

All the dinosaurs recommended in this book are listed in this classification scheme. Although palaeontologists differ in their ideas of dinosaur classification, this diagram should help you to see where your dinosaur fits in.

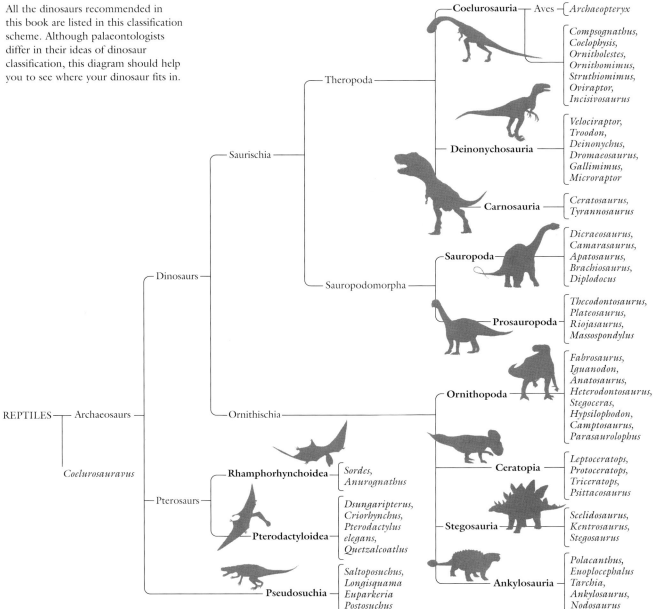

Retail Outlets

 Algeria
Brachiosaurus

Argentina
La Rioja province: *Riojasaurus*

 Australia
Northeast: *Thecodontosaurus*

Belgium
Bernissart Emporium:
Iguanodon

Brazil
**Santana Formation –
Pterosauros Brasileiras:**
Criorhynchus

 Canada
**Alberta – Alberta Dinomart,
Edmonton:** *Anatosaurus,
Ankylosaurus, Leptoceratops,
Parasaurolophus*
**Belly River Formation
Dancing School:** *Leptoceratops,
Stegoceras*
Red Deer River Retailers:
*Dromaeosaurus, Euoplocephalus,
Ornithomimus, Troodon,
Struthiomimus, Triceratops,*
Steveville Stenonychostore:
Troodon

China
**Inner Mongolia – Nemegt
Basin, Bath and Toilet Centre:**
Therizinosaurus
**Liaoning – Yixian formation
Trading House:** *Microraptor*
Rural markets: *Incisivosaurus,
Velociraptor*
Sinkiang Province:
Euoplocephalus, Dsungaripterus
Tibet – Lhasa Bazaar:
Ornithomimus

France
La Chassagne: *Plateosaurus*
Nice: *Compsognathus,
Euparkeria*

Germany
Bavaria – Beer Festivals:
Compsognathus, Euparkeria
**Riedenberg-Kelheim
Dinosauren:** *Compsognathus*
**Solnhofen – Archaeopteryx
Exchange:** *Anurognathus,
Archaeopteryx, Criorhynchus,
Pterodactylus*
Halberstadt: *Plateosaurus*
Nehden: *Iguanodon*
Trössingen: *Plateosaurus*

 Kazakhstan
Sordes
**Asian Feather-Farmers Co-
Operative:** *Therizinosaurus*

 Lesotho
Red Beds Fabrostore:
Fabrosaurus, Heterodontosaurus

Madagascar
Coelurosauravus

Mongolia
Bayn Shireh – horse markets:
Talarurus
Carnosaur Market:
Tyrannosaurus
Djadochta Markets:
Protoceratops, Velociraptor
Oshih Formation Company:
Psittacosaurus
Ulan Bator – horse markets:
*Gallimimus, Leptoceratops,
Oviraptor, Velociraptor*

 Portugal
Camptosaurus

Russia
**Transbaykalia – Asian Feather-
Farmers Co-Op:** *Therizinosaurus*

South Africa
Massospondylus
Cape Province:
Heterodontosaurus

 Switzerland
Plateosaurus

 Tanzania
**Tendaguru Hill Farm
Supplies:** *Brachiosaurus,
Dicraeosaurus, Kentrosaurus*

Turkestan
Longisquama

 U.K.
Bristol – Thecodontostore:
Thecodontosaurus
Charmouth: *Scelidosaurus*
Isle of Wight: *Hypsilophodon,
Polacanthus*
Kent: *Iguanodon*
**Oxfordshire – Cumnor
Dinomart:** *Camptosaurus*
Sussex: *Iguanodon*

U.S.A.
**Arizona – Arizona Anchisaurs
Inc:** *Massospondylus*
Petrified Forest –*Postosuchus*
**Colorado – Canyon City
Camarasaurs:** *Camarasaurus*
Dinosaur Depot: *Ornithomimus*
**Grand River Valley Dino
Depot:** *Brachiosaurus*
**Green Mountain Creek
Cresteds, Denver:** *Triceratops*
Fremont County – Quarry 1:
Stegosaurus, Ceratosaurus
Morrison Brontobooth:
Apatosaurus
Canyon City – M.P. Felch:
Diplodocus
**Fremont County – Trex
Quarry:** *Tyrannosaurus*
**Connecticut – Coelurosaur
Trading Center:** *Coelophysis*
**Kansas – Olde Worlde Dino
Shoppyne Center:** *Nodosaurus*
Montana – Dinomart:
*Ankylosaurus, Deinonychus,
Diplodocus, Ornithomimus,
Triceratops*

**Hell Creek KT Interface
Emporium:** *Tyrannosaurus,
Ankylosaurus*
**New Jersey Auto and Dino
Center:** *Anatosaurus,
Struthiomimus*
**New Mexico – Ghost Ranch
Theropods, Abiquiu:**
Coelophysis
Albuquerque Hadrostore:
Parasaurolophus
**Oklahoma – Acrocanthostore,
Atoka County:** *Apatosaurus*
Rogers Stegoshop:
*Apatosaurus, Camarasaurus,
Stegosaurus*
**South Dakota – Coyote
Camptos:** *Camptosaurus,
Triceratops*
Texas – Teerex Supplies:
Tyrannosaurus
Big Bend Big Birds:
Quetzalcoatlus
**Post Quarry Postosuchians
by Post:** *Postosuchus*
**Utah – Cleveland-Lloyd
Quarry:** *Tyrannosaurus*
**Dinosaur National Monument
Carnegie Museum Shop:**
Camarasaurus
Salt Lake Stegos: *Apatosaurus,
Camptosaurus, Diplodocus,
Stegosaurus*
**Wyoming – Bone Cabin
Quarry, Como:** *Ornitholestes,
Apatosaurus*
Como Bluff Brontocenter:
Apatosaurus, Camarasaurus
**Olde Worlde Dino Shoppynge
Center:** *Camptosaurus,
Nodosaurus, Ornitholestes*
Albany County – Quarry 13:
Stegosaurus
Albany County – Sheep Creek:
Diplodocus
Teerex Supplies: *Tyrannosaurus*
**Niobrara County –
Tricerashops:** *Triceratops*

 Zimbabwe
Zimbabwe Zoo Supplies:
Massospondylus

To Fabian

I would like to thank all those whose encouragement, knowledge and inspiration contributed to this book. I am especially grateful to Nic Cheetham, Richard Dawkins, Dougal Dixon, William Hopkinson and my wife Kaye.

First published in the United Kingdom in 1983 by André Deutsch Limited

This revised and updated edition first published in 2003 by Weidenfeld & Nicolson

This new edition first published in 2004 by Weidenfeld & Nicolson
Wellington House, 125 Strand
London, WC2R 0BB

Distributed in the United States of America by
Sterling Publishing Co., Inc.
387 Park Avenue South,
New York, NY 10016-8810

A CIP catalogue record for this book is available from the British Library
ISBN 0-297-84398-2

Printed and bound in Italy

The author and the publisher would like to thank the following dinosaur-keepers for their help:

Caroline Cambridge, Oliver Cambridge, Anthony Cheetham, James Cheetham, Ros Clark, Jamie Clifford, Amy Coombes, Dan Cornish, Mandy Courtney, Henry Hailstone, Susan Haynes, Aitken Rainbow Jolly, David Jones, Matt Lowing, Ella Matthews, Jake Mathews, Jane Matthews, Mae Matthews, Robin Matthews, Charlotte Millner, Amber Ponton, Nigel Soper.

No dinosaurs were harmed in the making of this book.

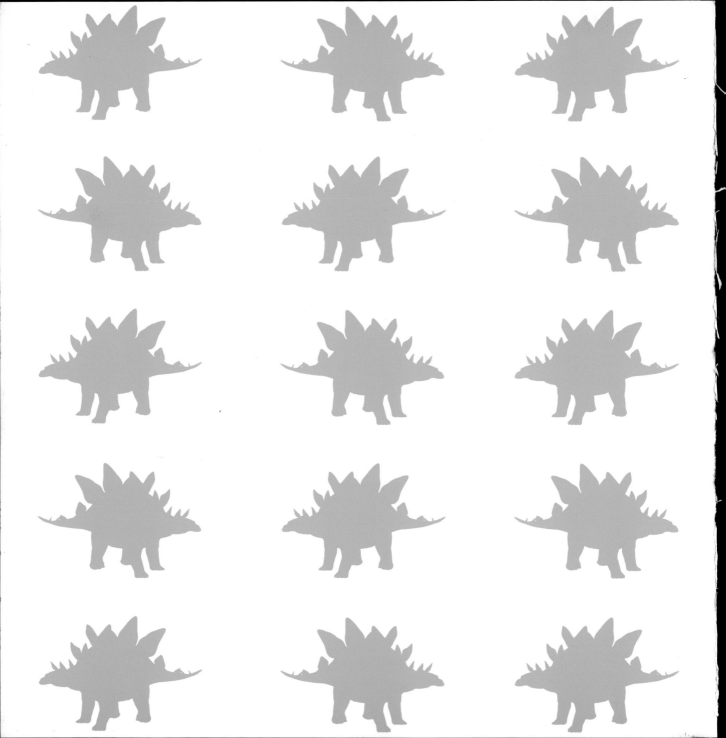